31 DAYS *or less!*

HOW TO RELIEVE STRESS, DECLUTTER & KEEP IT THAT WAY

EASY STEPS
to an
ORGANIZED
LIFE
IN 31 DAYS OR LESS

BY STEPHANIE WILSON

www.31daily.com

Requests for information should be addressed to:
31 Daily, 1567 Highland Dr NE, Ste 110-235 Issaquah, WA 98029
www.31daily.com

Library of Congress Cataloging-in-Publication Data
Wilson, Stephanie, author
Easy Steps to an Organized Life in 31 Days or Less/Stephanie Wilson
Pages cm
Print Book ISBN: 9781520273464

CONTENTS

INTRODUCTION

"Our life is frittered away by detail... simplify, simplify."

~Henry David Thoreau

An organized life yields a better, more productive and more peaceful life.

And living life looking outward will produce the greatest joy.

A joyful life, obviously, is a happy life.

I want to live a happy life – don't you?

The world is a crazy place, more demanding and complicated than ever before. It's not going to get better. Home should be a sanctuary, a peaceful respite in an unpredictable world.

But without organization, without a plan, home only serves yet another stressful component in our already busy lives.

Per a recent survey on behalf of the Huffington Post, clutter was the main culprit of home-related stress in survey respondents.

ACCUMULATION

Accumulation most often equals... clutter.

Nothing lends itself more to disorganization than clutter. And the older my family grows, the more we tend to accumulate.

It's not easy to part with things... and ways.

I'm a sentimentalist. Every "thing" in our home, to me, has a meaning, a memory, an emotion attached to it.

Learning to separate meaning from meaningless is the goal.

Here's the good news. Clearing the meaningless clutter from our life allows us to keep and enjoy what we love, what evokes memories and true meaning.

Nothing produces disharmony more than cluttered, disorganized stacks of meaningless accumulations.

ORGANIZATION

"The best way to get something done is to begin."

~ Author Unknown

Organizing your life might seem a bit overwhelming.

But I promise you, it's not!

It's simply one step in front of the other. Tackling one small project, after another, until in 31 days, you will find yourself ... simply organized. With a system and routine that will keep you that way for the rest of your life.

We not aiming at perfection. We're aiming at function. We're not pursuing process, we're pursuing a meaningful life with a home that supports peace and harmony.

31-DAY CHALLENGE

For the next 31 days, we'll post a brief daily challenge, with a checklist, to help you eliminate clutter, create and an organizational structure that works for you and your family. We'll create control areas to charge phones, put mail, find keys, create meal planning, homework, office work, and other needs. Places designed to carry out daily tasks.

At the end of 31 days, you'll have put your eyes on everything in your home. Some areas will be quick, others will take a bit of thought and a little more time, depending on your needs.

The result will be an in-place plan that you've designed, and customized to function for your life. A plan that can be adjusted and tweaked as life changes or addresses change. A method you'll want to revisit time and again.

And your life?

Clear, purposeful... organized.

Here's to simplifying life – in 31 days or less.

HOW

Are you ready to take control of your life and organize your home once and for all?

For the next 31 days, we will walk through each zone of your home and provide suggestions on eliminating clutter, organizing your space, and ideas on how to keep it that way.

And by the way, tomorrow, Day 1 of the challenge, is really easy.

Are you ready?

I certainly am!

Join me as together we reclaim peace in our lives!

DAY 1: TAKE A WALK

I promised you this was doable. I promised it was simply taking one step in front of the other!

Today's objective is easy.

TAKE A WALK

But before you do, I want you to...

Focus — on the goal

Eyes — on the reality of what is now

Pay Attention — to the details that will create a better tomorrow

Launching this kind of change will be monumental.

It can and will be life-changing if done purposefully.

Before you begin the effort of decluttering and organizing, take a few moments, in the center of your home... and close your eyes. Visualize not what you see, not what you feel, but what you want to see and feel. What kind of home do you want to live in? What does it look like? What does it feel like? What is the purpose?

Let that picture become crystal clear in your mind. **Don't forget it.**

As an example, it's incredibly important to me to feel space around me. I don't like to feel crowded. Yet I love to feel cozy and wrapped in warmth. Marrying the two is my challenge.

Think about the people who live with you. What are their needs, their struggles? What kind of space benefits them?

A FINAL THOUGHT

The *"things"* we surround ourselves with are temporal. We can find beauty in those "things." But we cannot find true...

joy. "Things" can be representative of moments in which we found joy, people who have brought joy, events that have brought joy. But the object itself does not bring joy.

I lived both with plenty and through times when things were tight financially. As most of us have. And through that, I've learned to hold life loosely. When I hold too tightly, life has a way of becoming challenging.

Possessions are temporal... transitory. They come and they go.

Clearing the clutter from our lives allows us to concentrate more fully on that which does matter.

Okay — moving on!

Grab a notebook and pencil – or the notes section of your phone and jot down what you see.

"The best way to get something done is to begin."

~ Author Unknown

WHAT TO KEEP IN MIND

1. A ZONE

I'm not an incredibly detailed person. I like broad strokes and general zones. That being said. All things must have a place where they belong. Clutter accumulates when it doesn't have a home. Every time. You're looking for zones today. General themes of use. Habits and patterns.

How are the areas in your home used... do they work? Or how can they function better?

2. A PURPOSE

Do the "things" taking up space in your home have a function? Is that function working, does it need to be tweaked, or eliminated entirely? Can it be re-purposed, moved or its use changed to accomplish flow in your home?

3. A MEANING

Of the accumulations, which of those are meaningful? And of those, which are the most meaningful? Do they tell a story about who and what you are and stand for as a family? Distinguish between items that are non-negotiable and those that could either be packed away or simply eliminated.

4. A FUNCTION

If it doesn't work. Eliminate it. No one has the time or energy to collect things that no longer function, work or are broken. They take up space. And space is a priceless premium. And, it interrupts your primary goal: a streamlined life and home.

5. A GUEST

Look at your home through the eyes of a guest if possible. We can become blind to our accumulations. Try to see your home through the eyes of a guest, a realtor, a friend who hasn't visited in a while. Try to see what they would see.

CHECKLIST

1. GO OUTSIDE

Walk into your home through the front door. The door that may not get a lot of use if you're like us!

With your notebook or list, proceed through your home, room by room, closet by closet.

2. TRAFFIC PATTERN

Mimic your family's daily traffic patterns. What happens when they walk through the door? Which Door? Where do they drop...

- shoes

- backpacks

- briefcases

- mail

- keys

- handbags

- clothing

3. WRITE IT DOWN

Make copious notes because patterns are sometimes easier to work with than fight against. You'll create zones in your home to accommodate these general patterns.

Make notes on items that aren't working, general repairs, maintenance issues, areas that need a little extra elbow grease. (Save those notes because they're for another day).

TOMORROW

Tomorrow, we'll create a Control Center. A launching pad. A zone that everyone passes through. This could be: a corner in the kitchen, a nook in a hallway, or a centrally located home office. It could even be near the interior garage door. Shelves are key. Designate that place today.

Supplies needed:

- a file box

- an information board — *(bulletin board, whiteboard or chalkboard)*

- magnetic clips

- calendars

- dry-erase markers

- push pins

DAY 2: CONTROL CENTER

A Control Center is simply your family's hub of information. A family cockpit... or launching pad. A place where information flows through and to.

WHAT IT IS...

Family calendars, sports schedules, weekly and monthly meal plans, grocery lists, to-do lists, maintenance notes *(like the ones you created yesterday on your walk)*, emergency information, important phone numbers, short-term school papers and forms, perhaps necessary medical records to keep at your fingertips... are all ideas appropriate for the Control Center.

WHAT IT ISN'T...

What it isn't... a drop zone.

This isn't the place to drop bulky items, like backpacks, briefcases... the place to toss magazines, circulars... the mail or other miscellaneous items that don't have a home.

To work effectively, it must stay completely organized and decluttered.

We are beginning our 31 Days of Organizing here because once the hub is functional, the other zones begin to take shape. And most importantly, once the needs are identified, we can eliminate that which isn't.

WHERE IT SHOULD BE...

Centrally located within your home's main traffic zone. Ideas for location could include; a corner in the kitchen, a nook in a hallway, or a centrally located home office. It could even be near the interior garage door. Shelves are key as is a wall to post a bulletin board, chalkboard, or a whiteboard, and most especially a calendar.

SUGGESTED TOOLS:

A shelf-size acrylic file folder *(Container Store has these for around $25)*. Purchase color-coded hanging files. Code or labels these files by family member or category, whichever makes the most sense to you. Perhaps a bill file, a school file, a social file — this is the place for "floating" papers.

Household binders that include regular use instruction manuals, maintenance notes, etc.

Bulletin board to post important invitations, school class schedules, verses or motivating quotes, tickets to an upcoming event or a sentimental greeting card. Keep it neat and tidy in a grid-like pattern to keep it functioning and streamlined.

Phone/Tablet Charging Station – I especially like this for kids. The cords are hidden, and the phones are not in their rooms.

CHECKLIST

Objective: *to create a control center centrally located in your home.*

Once you've identified where your Control Center will be...

- ☐ Gather your supplies appropriate to your choice of bulletin board, whiteboard or chalkboard: magnetic clips, calendars, dry-erase markers, and push pins.

- ☐ Hang your boards, post menus, calendars and other essential information.

- ☐ Place your identified files on a nearby shelf.

- ☐ Fill in your calendar.

- ☐ Post at least tonight's dinner. We have posted some resources online at:

  http://www.31daily.com/simply-solving-the-whats-for-dinner-dilemma-a-meal-plan/

TOMORROW

Your Front Entry Foyer.

We'll clean, declutter... and repurpose!

CONTROL CENTER INSPIRATION

Hobby Lobby, Pottery Barn, Howtonestforless.com, ciburbanity.com

DAY 3: FRONT ENTRY FOYER

The Welcome

It's appropriate to begin in the entry, the first room that welcomes you home and last room you see before heading out the door.

What is the first thing you see? What is the first thing... you want to see?

Today we'll be strategic with all the items that somehow find their home in the entry... and do a little cleaning as well.

By the time you're done, you'll have to treat yourself with a cup of coffee just for an excuse to leave and then return — through your newly organized and cleaned Front Entry Foyer!

OBJECTIVE: FRONT ENTRY FOYER

The Front Door Entry is one of the most revealing parts of your home. You want it to be welcoming, but it can also be a grand central station! A perfect drop zone. An area that can attract all kinds of bulky clutter. We can fix that.

Depending on how many entries you have, this can be the catchall place for keys, shoes, mail, backpacks, handbags... coats, and so on.

MAKING CHOICES

It's time to clear the clutter and make your entry function for you.

The primary focus today is to give everything that needs to be in your entry a home. A place that makes sense. If keys are kept here, a cute dish or hook or wire container might be appropriate. What about shoes, handbags, and umbrellas?

Or is there another spot that these items could be relocated to — and that people will use.

In our home, the Control Center is centrally located in a small desk nestled in our kitchen. As it is the hub of our home, it's a natural location for keys, etc. As for shoes, jackets, umbrellas — we've set up a small bench inside the garage with storage underneath for shoes, pegs overhead for jackets, and hats. Backpacks go to designated study areas.

Could that be a solution for you?

Today is a day to be creative and strategic! I'd love to hear how you solved some of your entry dilemmas!

At the bottom of this post are some great inspirations!

CHECKLIST

Objective: *to create a pleasant, organized and functional entry.*

- ☐ Assess what needs to be kept near the front door, organize it, and contain it in attractive containers that fit with the decor of your home. Everything else that isn't essential or that makes a statement for your home should be removed.

☐ If you have a chair that tends to invite clutter — consider moving and repurposing it.

☐ After everything that can be moved is cleared — it's the perfect time to clean!

☐ Vacuum every corner, including area rugs, and dust the floorboards. You'll be so happy you did!

☐ Using an extended duster, run it up the corners of the room.

☐ Dust any pieces of furniture, most especially entry consoles. Which, if they have drawers, make excellent places for things like keys, etc.

☐ If you have any windows, use a bit of glass cleaner.

☐ Finally, don't neglect the front door! Thoroughly dust and/or wash it.

☐ Put some thought into where you're going to place relocated items. You don't want to handle them more than once. Plan today for where their new home will be.

TOMORROW

Moving into the kitchen. We'll clean, declutter... and eliminate!

FRONT ENTRY INSPIRATIONS

Molly Frey Design, Hometalk.com, Designertrapped.com

DAY 4: KITCHEN COUNTERTOPS

Today we'll begin in one of my favorite rooms in the house — the kitchen!

Often penned in vintage cookbooks, you'll find this little prayer:

"So bless my little kitchen, God,
And those who enter in,
May they find naught but
Joy and Peace,
and Happiness therein."

- M. Peterson (1944)

Kitchens have been said to be the heart of every home. A cozy room filled with warmth and fun and community... and tantalizing aromas. A room that nourishes both the body and the soul.

A gathering room for todays' families, kitchens bring the concept of multi-task to whole new levels. Everything from food prep and storage to homework and meals, entertaining to family meetings happen very often in this room.

Another motivating factor to keeping your kitchen functioning well is that they are a key component of your home's value.

Trulia, an online real estate listing service, says that there are two rooms that sell every home — a well-appointed kitchen and the master bath. "A well-appointed kitchen will dramatically increase the value of your home, so it's worth spicing up yours to grab buyer attention." We'll get to the master later this month. But we'll begin tackling the kitchen today!

OBJECTIVE: KITCHEN COUNTERS AND UTENSILS DRAWERS

Kitchens have a way of becoming unruly — quickly. It may be the most used room in your home, it certainly is in mine.

For that reason, we are splitting the kitchen area into 4 days — 5 if you count the junk drawer.

Day 4: Kitchen Counters and Utensils Drawers

Day 5: Cupboards and Drawers

Day 6: Pantry

Day 7: Refrigerator

Day 8: A Junk Drawer

Kitchens are a magnet for clutter. Between the have-to-have gadgets we buy ourselves and the gifts we receive from loving friends and family who know we like to cook, it can become overwhelming to keep it clutter free. It's easy to rationalize the clutter because after all, kitchen gadgets can be expensive. And the broken ones sometimes aren't really that broken. They might come in handy one day. I'm smiling! I've heard that same voice in my head too!

UTENSILS

Today we'll take a hard look at our utensils.

To successfully manage, declutter and organize our kitchen spaces, we probably have items we need to be eliminated. Here's the criteria: discard any utensil or gadget that is broken, never used nor truthfully likely to be, or that we have multiples of or exact replicas.

KITCHEN COUNTERS

Whether you have ample counter space in your kitchen or not, those flat surfaces seem to attract a lot of clutter. Keeping them neat and organized is a challenge.

Removing everything that doesn't get daily use is one trick to keep counters tidy and neatly organized. Another is to always corral items, especially small things, in a container. And finally, when finished using the item, put it back where it belongs– quickly!

Take a hard look at the appliances you have sitting on your countertops and determine how often you use them.

Daily use appliances that remain on my counters are;

the coffee pot

the electric mixer *(it's too heavy to move and it gets regular use)*

 a toaster

• a teapot

• a silver tray with salt, peppercorns, and olive oil

• my knife block.

I try to keep everything else hidden when not in use.

CHECKLIST

☐ Remove all the utensils from their drawers and put them on the counter.

☐ Clean and discard as appropriate.

☐ Wipe out the drawer and flatware/knife holders and return the remaining utensils.

☐ **Good job! You've just jumpstarted tomorrow's challenge by taking care of these drawers!**

☐ Find new homes for non-daily or irregularly used appliances if possible. Discard any that aren't working.

☐ Group appliances with like items and functions.

☐ Thoroughly wipe down countertops, corners and under remaining appliances.

☐ Items to be tossed or donated, remove to a box — out of sight!

TOMORROW

Kitchen cupboards and drawers

ORGANIZED KITCHEN COUNTERTOP INSPIRATIONS

Martha Stewart, MakingHomeBase.com, Domino.com,
Mittogvaarthjem.blogspot.nl

DAY 5: KITCHEN CUPBOARD & DRAWERS

"Your personal work style will determine where you store and use the items in your kitchen, but the goal is to get that room and its contents to serve your needs as smoothly and efficiently as possible. If you invest the time and energy into decluttering and organizing your kitchen, it is an investment that will pay off in happiness for years to come," says organizational expert Monica Ricci.

Yesterday, we cleaned, decluttered, and organized kitchen counters and utensil drawers. Today we'll tackle the remaining cupboards and drawers.

SCHEDULE

The kitchen area will be split into 5 days. Very doable!

Day 4: Kitchen Counters and Utensils Drawers

Day 5: Cupboards and Drawers (today)

Day 6: Pantry

Day 7: Refrigerator

Day 8: A Junk Drawer

OBJECTIVE: KITCHEN CUPBOARDS AND DRAWERS

Today will be about strategic space planning and reorganization. We'll look at workflow, at new ways to use vertical space, and declutter. There are some excellent ideas at the bottom of this post.

As you assess what's in each cupboard and drawer — remember to discard anything that is:

- broken

- never used or likely to be used

- you have multiples of that are similar

Tomorrow we'll be working with the pantry or food cupboard so skip food-related spaces today.

CHECKLIST

Objective: *Clean and declutter nonfood-related cupboards, cabinets, and drawers.*

- ☐ Empty cabinets.

- ☐ Eliminate items that are broken, unused, or not likely to be used. Remember, space is a premium.

- ☐ Sort items and group per use (baking items, cookware, seasonal, special occasion). Everyday items like glasses, plates, and utensils should be in accessible cabinets, heavy cookware in bottom cabinets and seasonal or fragile items in harder to access upper cabinets.

- ☐ Create storage in clear labeled containers or bins and group small items together.

- ☐ Organize cabinets per use. Locate cookware close to where you do food prep, glasses near the sink, etc.

- ☐ For small space areas, get creative with vertical storage. Ideas might include hooks for mugs, lazy

Susan's, and vertical storage attachments on the back of cabinet doors.

☐ Wipe out cupboards inside and out, from top to bottom, and return organized items to appropriate cabinets or drawers.

TOMORROW

Kitchen Pantry

ORGANIZED KITCHEN CUPBOARD INSPIRATIONS

Real Simple Magazine, House Beautiful, Martha Stewart, IKEA

DAY 6: THE PANTRY

"A well-stocked pantry helps you think creatively about how to feed yourself and anyone who happens to be with you, a thoughtfully prepared, flavorful, and wholesome meal... A familiar pantry is like being surrounded by friends who won't let you down, within instant reach."

~ Alice Waters, author

Yesterday, we cleaned, decluttered, and organized kitchen cupboard and drawers. The work invested yesterday will reap tomorrow's rewards. When I open my organized and tidy cupboards, even on the most hectic days, everything seems easier and more possible.

SCHEDULE

As you know, the kitchen area will be split into 5 days.

Day 4: Kitchen Counters and Utensils Drawers

Day 5: Cupboards and Drawers

Day 6: Pantry (today)

Day 7: Refrigerator

Day 8: A Junk Drawer

OBJECTIVE

An organized pantry is a relief when it's time for dinner meal prep. It can also be a lifesaver when planned meals go awry and pantry staple dinners are a must. Organizing it strategically with clear labels and zones will help keep it that way.

While it seems profitable to organize items in a pantry by size, grouping in zones help keep food organized, meal prep simple, and grocery shopping easy.

For some inspiring ideas, be sure to check out the photos at the bottom of this post.

ZONES

Zone ideas: Pick and choose according to lifestyle and family need.

- ## COOKING & SPICE ZONE

A zone for seasonings, spices, and oils. A lazy Susan or dedicated drawer can be a space saver for spices.

- ## BAKING ZONE

Stocked with clear, airtight containers for flour, sugar, mixes, frostings, dried fruit, etc.

- ## GENERAL FOOD ZONE

A zone for canned foods, organized by type (soup, veggies, fruit, broth, etc.) and then size. Consider a stair-step shelf to keep items in easy view.

- ## LUNCH ZONE

Store items in this zone that pertain to quick and brown bag lunches. A basket or bin could hold various size baggies, lunch sacks, twist ties, plastic utensils. Also, a great location for quick fix meals like macaroni and cheese, etc.

- **BREAKFAST ZONE**

Foods relating to breakfast should be kept in this zone; boxed and instant cereals, breakfast drinks, bagels, crumpets, etc. Easy to grab on busy mornings.

- **SNACK ZONE**

For me this consists of a portable container, in my case a basket with handles, that contains snacking foods (individual size chips, microwave popcorn, nuts, dried fruit, etc.). When kids visit, or hungry people begin grazing and raiding the pantry or refrigerator, this portable snack bin is perfect.

- **BREAD ZONE**

I use a large shallow basket to keep breads within easy reach.

- **BEVERAGE ZONE**

Coffee, tea, drink packets, and beverage condiments.

CHECKLIST

Objective: *To organize and divide pantry into zones to keep food organized and meal prep simple. Keep everything labeled and visible, small items contained.*

☐ Empty pantry and dust from the highest to the lowest shelf.

☐ Eliminate clutter, broken containers, empty wrappers and expired food items.

☐ Determine zones that fit lifestyle and pantry size and designate an area for each. Frequently used zones should be in easy-to-reach locations.

☐ Organize and group small items in appropriate containers.

☐ Install any portable or hardware organizational units.

☐ Group foods into appropriate zones and locations and place in the pantry.

TOMORROW

Refrigerator

ORGANIZED PANTRY INSPIRATIONS

HGTV, Arianna Belle, Amazon.com, A Thousand Words

DAY 7: THE REFRIGERATOR

OBJECTIVE:

Yesterday, we cleaned and organized the pantry. To any home cook, an organized pantry is a relief for meal prep, meal planning, and grocery shopping. The same is true for the refrigerator.

The refrigerator, however, has an added component — food safety and freshness. It's not just organizing to be pretty and efficient, it's organizing to keep food safe and fresher longer.

And as always, there's a method. A simple 5-Step method — we'll walk you through that guide. Be sure to watch the video near the end of the post.

SCHEDULE

As you know, the kitchen area will be split into 5 days.

Day 4: Kitchen Counters and Utensils Drawers

Day 5: Cupboards and Drawers

Day 6: Pantry

Day 7: Refrigerator *(today)*

Day 8: A Junk Drawer

FOOD SAFETY

The FDA advises home refrigerators should be kept at 40 °F or below and the freezer at 0 °F. They also recommend purchasing an inexpensive refrigerator thermometer for both the refrigerator and freezer to monitor cold temps, and to check them often.

FDA REFRIGERATOR STRATEGIES: KEEPING FOOD SAFE

In addition to keeping the temperature in your fridge at 40 °F, you can take additional steps to make sure your refrigerated foods stay as safe as possible.

Avoid "Overpacking." Cold air must circulate around refrigerated foods to keep them properly chilled.

Wipe Up Spills Immediately to Avoid Cross-Contamination.

Keep It Covered.

Check Expiration Dates on Foods.

Clean the Fridge Out Frequently.

HOW LONG CAN I KEEP FOOD IN THE REFRIGERATOR?

The FDA has produced a handy guide, which I keep in my "Control Center," in my household notebook. Print it off for a handy reference.

Online Resource: Refrigerator Storage Chart on our website: http://www.31daily.com/wp-content/uploads/2016/09/31Daily-FDA-A-Z-Guide-Refrigerator-Storage-Chart.pdf

Or the FoodKeeper App from FoodSafety.gov

5-STEP GUIDE TO REFRIGERATOR ORGANIZATION

1.THE DOOR

The door is the warmest part of the refrigerator. So, foods that require the lowest temperatures should be kept here. That includes most condiments, butter and cheese. Eggs and milk require colder temperatures and should not be kept in the door.

- Butter

- Condiments

- Juice

- Cooking oils

- Soda

- Water

2.THE COOKED MEAT/DELI BIN

This storage option is most common on French-door bottom-freezers, where it typically sits beneath the crisper drawers. Items belonging in this area are:

- Bacon

- Bacon

- Cheeses

- Deli meats

- Hot dogs

3.THE DRAWERS

On many refrigerators, there are at least two drawers dedicated to fruits and vegetables, with adjustable humidity levels. Dedicate one drawer to each and adjust the humidity level from low to high.

- Fruit Drawer: Low-Humidity

- Vegetable Drawer: High-Humidity

4.THE LOWER SHELF

The lower shelf, usually located in the middle of the fridge, is the coldest part of the refrigerator. This makes it ideal for storage of items that are more susceptible to developing harmful bacteria, including the following:

- Eggs (in their original carton)

- Milk – Toward the back of the refrigerator

- Raw fish, meat, and poultry (on trays to catch drippings so as not to contaminate other foods)

5. THE UPPER SHELF

The upper shelves, conversely, are the warmest part, with temperatures often reaching up around 40 °F. Leftovers, drinks, and ready-to-eat foods (like yogurt, cheese, and deli meats). That's too warm for milk and eggs, though yogurt is okay because it's fermented. Here's the complete list of what to store on the top shelf.

- Jam & Jelly

- Leftovers

- Peanut butter

- Snacks (like hummus and fruit cups)

- Yogurt and other ready-to-eat foods (like cheese, deli meats)

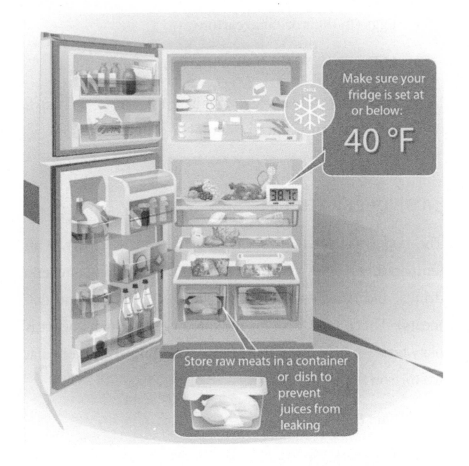

CHECKLIST

Objective: *To clean and organize the refrigerator and freezer — following the food safety 5-Step Guide — to keep food fresh, safe, and accessible.*

- [ ] Remove food and place on a counter or in a cooler. Check dates on packaged foods and discard expired items.

- [ ] Remove shelves and drawers and set in the sink.

- [ ] To clean and eliminate odors: mix a solution of 2 tablespoons baking soda to 1-quart hot water and wipe down the interior. Dry thoroughly.

- [ ] Clean the shelves and drawers with the same solution, dry thoroughly and return to the refrigerator.

- [ ] Wipe down the outside of the refrigerator, including the top.

- [ ] Return food to the refrigerator, placing them according to the 5-Step Refrigerator Guide.

- [ ] Repeat steps with the freezer.

TOMORROW

A Junk Drawer

ORGANIZED
REFRIGERATOR INSPIRATIONS

Container Store,

DAY 8: JUNK DRAWER

The junk drawer. For many, a time capsule, artifacts from days gone by. Little tidbits of collections, pieces of memorabilia we're loath to let go — a repository of meaningless items that may have no significance other than they may, someday, be useful.

That is the junk drawer. The drawer of detritus.

You can tell a lot about a person or a family from the household junk drawer. "I snoop through people's drawers, pantries, closets and garages as part of my research," says Kit Yarrow, a consumer psychologist at Golden Gate University, "and I can say without hesitation that the junk drawer is the most revealing place I can look," she told NPR in a 2014 online article.

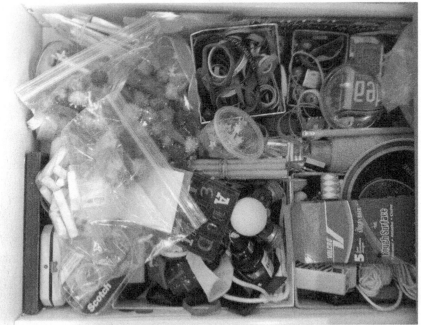

A junk drawer in Massachusetts. Mish/Flickr

And then, she says, "it gets interesting, because what people also store in junk drawers are things they can't part with, but don't use — like vacation mementos and love notes." Puzzle pieces of the past.

OBJECTIVE

We know what they are — the question remains, what to do with it? It's not a lost cause.

6 TIPS FOR TAMING THE JUNK DRAWER

1. TAKE AN INVENTORY

Empty the contents of the drawer. In fact, take the whole drawer out and have a trash bag accessible. This is the time to eliminate expired coupons, scraps of paper that have no meaning — phone numbers to unnamed people (that's what I found!). Clear everything you can clear!

2. SORT INTO PILES

Sort things that don't belong and set aside: screws that go in the toolbox, tweezers that belong in the medicine kit, etc. For everything that stays, group like items together. Eliminate broken and duplicates, as always. Create piles of paper clips, rubber bands, hair clips, thumb tacks and so on.

3. TAME PAPER

"If you find that you still need some of the paper mess that has accumulated, consider adding plastic paper sleeves to the inside of one of your cabinet doors. It will take up relatively no space and still allow you to hold on to your favorite hand-written recipes and instruction booklets. Of course, keep in mind that most take-out menus and instruction booklets can be found online, which will save even more space," advises HGTV.

4. MAKE IT PRETTY

It's human nature to want to keep something beautiful. Consider lining your drawer with a pretty liner. It just might inspire you to keep it that way.

5. DIVIDE IT UP

Here's where you can get creative, save some money, and create usable dividers from common household items. Create dividers from business card holders, box tops, cereal boxes cut to size, cartons, old muffin tins or ice cube trays are innovative ways to divide and conquer the clutter.

6. KEEP WHAT MATTERS

While we're on a quest to simplify. Keep what matters. That memorabilia you haven't been able to part with. Those tidbits of the past. Create a memory box specifically for those items. And as the days grow cold and you're feeling a bit nostalgic, retrieve the box and tell the stories of your past.

USEFUL ITEMS FOR A JUNK DRAWER

HGTV Magazine featured an article in their October 2016 issue of 15 items every junk drawer should have. Here are 5 of the most useful items available at home improvement stores or Amazon.com.

1. Hem Tape, Scotch Essentials

2. Furniture Pencils, Minwax Blend-Fil (assorted colors)

3. Eyeglass Repair Kit

4. Household Battery Tester

5. Staple-Free Stapler

CHECKLIST

Objective*: To tame the junk drawer, making it a usable storage solution.*

☐ Remove the drawer.

☐ From the contents, set aside all items that belong elsewhere: screws for the toolbox and so on.

☐ For that which stays, divide into piles of like items.

☐ Discard what can be eliminated (expired coupons, scraps of paper and so on).

☐ Wipe out the drawer and line it.

☐ Create usable dividers that fit the drawer and correspond to your "keep piles."

☐ Return items to the newly organized drawer.

☐ Return items have that have another home.

☐ Create a memory box for memorabilia you want to keep.

TOMORROW

Eating Areas

JUNK DRAWER INSPIRATIONS

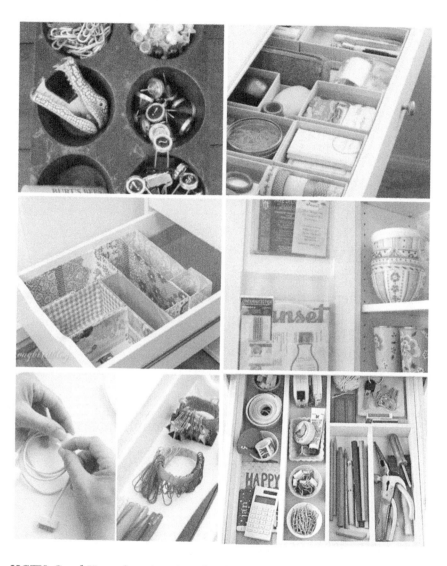

HGTV, Good Housekeeping, Songbird, Better Homes & Gardens

DAY 9: EATING AREAS

OBJECTIVE

If the kitchen is the heart of the home... then the eating areas, the dining areas might be said to be the pulse of the home, the rhythm of the home.

Family tables are a gathering point.

Picture for a moment what happens at family tables:

- meals

- family game nights

- late night homework

- early morning devotions

- Super Bowl parties

- holiday celebrations

- family meetings

Are these relevant or revolutionary thoughts? Maybe...

"They hardly look like radicals, but nearly 400 Minneapolis parents did something revolutionary recently: they pledged to eat meals with their families at least four nights a week. 'Funny, isn't it, that you're being countercultural these days when you sit down to dinner?' muses William Doherty, Ph.D., director of the Marriage and Family Therapy Program at the University of Minnesota." ~The Family Table, 31Daily

Here's to being countercultural. I never thought I'd say that!

In the same article, we resourced data that showed children who ate regularly with their families tended to have higher grade-point averages, were more well-adjusted, less likely to feel depressed, suicidal, or smoke or use alcohol.

In a nutshell, that's why the eating area is incredibly important. I'm kind of passionate about this. It's important, vital even for the health of families. It's got to be a priority.

And to become a priority, it takes a little effort.

Yet, these areas sometimes must serve a dual purpose and therefore can accumulate clutter.

Let's do it! Remove the clutter, contain what needs to be contained... and re-create a "family table!" (View the images at the bottom of the post for some inspiration!)

CHECKLIST

Objective*: To create a functional family table — to promote fun, family memories.*

- ☐ De-clutter. Remove all items that don't belong and put them where they do. Leave only items that will be used in this space.

- ☐ Create a family table. If you don't already have an eating table, consider buying one, setting up a card table draped with a pretty cloth or quilt or obtain one second hand. Make it a priority to set up that family table.

- ☐ Dust all surfaces of furniture in this area, including overhead light fixtures.

- ☐ Vacuum, especially under the table.

- ☐ Launder any linens you use in this area.

- ☐ Create dedicated storage (furniture items with compartments that can hide these items are ideal) for items that must remain in this area.

☐ Clean and de-clutter any other eating surfaces you may have like an eating bar in the kitchen or a kitchen table.

☐ Celebrate with a family dinner or invite someone over for dessert and show off your newly cleaned room!

TOMORROW

The Living Room

EATING AREA INSPIRATIONS

Find what functions, make it beautiful... and make it you!

Julie Blanner, The Wood Grain Cottage, Driven by Decor

DAY 10: LIVING ROOMS

OBJECTIVE

A living room or family room is the room that collects and showcases the best of who you are as a family. A place to gather, have fun, relax, mingle and show hospitality. An intimate room that should warm and invigorate and above all, be functional.

Look at your room with fresh eyes, consult the list you made during your walk on Day 1.

The goal is to eliminate anything that detracts from the best of who you are.

Clutter can be beautiful trinkets, photos, books, magazines, collections as well as items accumulated with other places to call home, or those without a home.

The idea today is to pair back, contain, and showcase.

Take a look at your living room layout. Does it invite conversation? If family game nights happen here... is there a dedicated place?

Is there furniture no longer in use that could be eliminated to repurpose that space for something else?

For ideas on room layout and makeovers, Real Simple magazine has compiled 14 before and after photos that showcase some great ideas for warming up living spaces by simply rearranging furniture.

The living room does have its share of clutter challenges. Remote controls, DVDs, magazines, books, photos, etc. Create attractive storage for items that will stay in the living room. Like, baskets or trays for controllers and so on.

Finally, and most importantly, showcase items that tell the story of your family. There are some inspirational photos to give you some ideas.

When the room is finished... celebrate with a family movie night, game night, or invite some of your neighbors in for coffee!

CHECKLIST

Objective: To pair back unnecessary clutter, create functional and attractive storage for small items and showcase who you are.

☐ Clear the room of everything that belongs elsewhere and put it there.

☐ Make piles of magazines, newspapers, books, controllers, etc. Anything that is sitting on surfaces. Set them aside and out of the room.

☐ Consider furniture arrangement and whether it promotes conversation and flow in the room. If not, rearrange the pieces, even removing some, until you like the way it feels.

☐ Thoroughly dust all surfaces, including electronics that stay in the room, artificial plants, blinds, bookshelves, books, etc.

☐ Vacuum every corner, behind and under furniture that can be moved.

☐ If you have bookshelves or mantels, take a hard look at what can be removed, and what can be showcased. Fewer items displayed together in collections of 3-5 pieces are always the most attractive.

☐ Retrieve the items you previously set aside. Sort and create functional contained storage. Create designated areas for these small items.

☐ Celebrate your new room!

TOMORROW

Home Office

LIVING ROOM INSPIRATIONS

Eldorado Stone, Kelleynan, Pottery Barn

DAY 11: HOME OFFICE

If a home had an engine — it would be the home office. Most especially if you work from home, but even if not, it's incredibly important to an organized life to have a dedicated space to conduct life's business.

Different from a Control Center, the office is a dedicated resource room or space to conduct business, stock office and homework supplies, and so on.

If you don't have a dedicated room for a home office, there are easy ways to creatively set up a dedicated space within your home.

Simple ideas could be:

- an awkward nook

- a hallway

- a guestroom

- a guestroom

- an unused closet

- a corner of the living room

The last resort would be your bedroom, which should be your haven. Merely having office work in that room brings an element of stress best avoided if possible.

Today, we'll create or organize (if you already have an office) a computer station, printing station, a location for hanging files, and a place for office supplies.

CALENDAR

The office area is so important that we've split it up into 4 days as follows:

Day 11: The Office (today)

Day 12: Creating a Filing System

Day 13: Organizing Important Papers and Documents

Day 14: Creating a Mail Station

OFFICE SUPPLIES

Experts recommend that office supplies be kept out of sight. To maintain a clutter-free environment, supplies should be grouped by category, organized into containers that keeps them out of sight. Closets, shelves, bins, etc. are great locations. Creating functional storage by category is important. My favorite way to store supplies is in labeled plastic containers we stock on shelves in the office closet.

Important tool: Label Maker
There are so many good label makers. I have a Brother P-Touch and it's one of my favorite tools.

CATEGORIES FOR SUPPLY STORAGE

Depending on your office needs, like if you have kids in school, are some common categories for supply bins. Label each container:

- Writing Tools (markets, pens, pencils, erasers)

- Mail Tools (stamps, envelopes, labels)

- Budget (checkbook, blank checks, calculator)

- Notebooks (spiral, composition)

- Office Tools (stapler, staple remover, hole punch)

- Miscellaneous (index notecards, post-it-notes, glue, file tabs, etc.)

CHECKLIST

Objective: *Take simple steps to create space, declutter your office, and organize your supplies for effective life management.*

☐ If you don't already have a dedicated office, create a space for a computer station, printer station, hanging files and office supplies.

☐ Determine what is working about your current set up and what isn't. Endeavor to change what isn't working.

☐ Clear the desk and shelf surfaces. Sort contents in groups of like materials (bills, CD's and empty binders, files, books, and so on) and place them individual boxes. Set aside. (You'll be working with files tomorrow).

☐ Create a computer station.

☐ Create a printing station. If you have a wireless printer, it doesn't have to be near the desktop or laptop. Create a place for printing supplies; ink, paper, and so on).

☐ Sort and store office supplies in containers and label. Utilize baskets, bins, or my favorite, labeled plastic storage containers.

Keeping on top of office organization is an active project. Every day, day in and day out. To keep your newly organized space functioning, set aside 10 minutes at the end of every day to clear your desk, put supplies away, and ready the space for tomorrow activities.

TOMORROW

Creating a Filing System

OFFICE INSPIRATIONS

Homebunch.com, Loombrand.com, Real Simple, Theeverygirl.com

DAY 12: FILING SYSTEM

OBJECTIVE: TO CREAT A HOUSEHOLD FILING SYSTEM

Paper clutter can be overwhelming. Piles of paper tend to multiply and take over the best organizational intentions. To conquer it, you need a simple household filing system.

Setting up a filing system gives paper piles a home. It also allows you to find important documents at a moment's notice. A retrieval or archival repository.

The key to success? Purge, categorize and file.

3 KINDS OF FILES

ACTION FILES

Daily or weekly use files. Usually kept in an expandable file, a tabletop file box or rack and contain action items. Action items would include; bills, short-term works in progress, correspondence and so on.

WORKING FILES

Medium-term filing. These documents should be kept in a file cabinet, office desk drawer or cabinet. Working files would include; employment records, employment benefits, insurance records, bill statements, bank statements, working tax files (archived after 3 years), medical information, home maintenance, receipts, manuals and warranties, education information such as transcripts, diplomas, etc. and an inventory of your safe deposit box.

ARCHIVED FILES

Long-term filing that may be kept in a safe, a bank safe deposit box or other secure location. These documents would include; income tax returns, real estate documents and receipts, insurance policies, automobile documents, and warranties.

For more information on what to keep in files, visit this webpage:

https://publications.usa.gov/epublications/keeprecords/keeprecords.htm

A FILING SYSTEM

Color-code the household filing system. Color-coded files are visual labels that increase efficiency both in filing and retrieving. A well-organized filing system is one that allows you to retrieve the information you need as quickly and easily as possible. To keep it simple, consider buying color-coded hanging files to organize information into 5 unique categories that might look like this:

- Green – Financial

- Red – Medical

- Yellow – Insurance

- Orange – Personal Files

- Blue – House Files

COMMON FILE CATEGORIES

Automobile: maintenance records, repairs, lease statements, warranties.

Banking: banking files for all accounts.

Bills and loans: split into either category or by name of payee.

Health and healthcare: bills, individual family health records, and so on.

Housing: mortgage files, repairs, receipts.

Insurance: set up by name of insurer or by category – Homeowners, Life, Automobile.

Legal

Retirement

Valuables: appraisals, inventories and so on.

CALENDAR

The office area is so important that we've split it up into 4 days as follows:

- **Day 11**: The Office
- **Day 12**: Creating a Filing System *(today)*
- **Day 13**: Organizing Important Papers and Original Documents
- **Day 14**: Creating a Mail Station

CHECKLIST

Objective: Create a household filing system to eliminate paper clutter, easily access important documents and efficiently manage information.

☐ Identify locations for filing systems and create spaces for 3 types of files: action, working and archival.

☐ Sort existing paper and files into categories that make sense for your lifestyle. Ideas: financial, medical, insurance, vehicles, household, education etc.

☐ As you come across original documents (birth, marriage certificates, titles, estate files, and so on), scan for a backup digital file.

☐ Purge and shred all unnecessary paper.

☐ Sort paper and documents into labeled files and put in place.

TOMORROW

Organizing Important Papers and Original Documents

DAY 13: IMPORTANT DOCUMENTS

OBJECTIVE: ORGANIZING IMPORTANT PAPERS AND ORIGINAL DOCUMENTS

Nothing seems to accumulate faster than paper in a household. Between junk mail, important mail, not important mail, record paper, work paper, school paper, flyers, business cards, maps...

Do you ever get exasperated by all the paper? I know you do, and so do I.

A lot of paper isn't important, or has short-term importance, but some papers are incredibly important with lasting significance. Knowing what to keep and for how long and what to toss... and **where to put what** is the focus today.

Yesterday, we began to set up a household filing system.

Today, we'll dive a bit deeper and look at archival documents that should be kept in a household safe and what should be kept in a safe deposit box.

CALENDAR

The office area is so important that we've split it up into 4 days as follows:

- **Day 11**: The Office
- **Day 12**: Creating a Filing System

- **Day 13**: Organizing Important Papers and Original Documents *(today)*
- **Day 14**: Creating a Mail Station

A PAPER TIMELINE

In 2016, Consumer Reports *(http://www.consumerreports.org/taxes/how-long-to-keep-tax-documents)* recommended the following timeline for retaining important documents.

UNDER A YEAR

In this file, store your ATM, bank-deposit, and credit-card receipts until you reconcile them with your monthly statements. Once you've done that, shred the paper documents (to avoid ID theft) or securely trash electronic files unless you need them to support your tax return. Keep insurance policies and investment statements until new ones arrive.

1 YEAR PLUS

You'll want to hold onto loan documents until the loan is paid off. That will often be for more than a year. Then toss those papers out. If you own one or more vehicles hold onto the titles until you sell them. If you have investments in stocks, bonds, mutual funds or anything else, keep the investment purchase confirmations until you sell the investment so you can establish your cost basis and holding period. (If that information appears on your annual statements, you can keep those instead.)

7 YEARS

If you fail to report more than 25 percent of your gross income on your tax returns, the government has six years to collect the tax or start legal proceedings. So, when it comes to determining how long to keep tax records—electronic and paper— we recommend seven years, just in case. Also, hold on to employment records, W2s and 1099s, tax receipts, tax deduction and donation receipts.

FOREVER

Essential records such as birth and death certificates, marriage licenses, divorce decrees, Social Security cards, and military discharge papers should be kept indefinitely. Also, hold on to defined-benefit plan documents, estate-planning documents, life-insurance policies, and an inventory of your bank safe-deposit box (share a copy with your executor or your attorney).

SAFE DEPOSIT BOXES

A safe deposit box is considered the safest place to put important documents that are not easily replaced. However, "you should not store items you might need on short notice or in an emergency, says Lawrence Lehmann, partner in the law firm Lehmann Norman & Marcus in New Orleans, and president of the National Association of Estate Planners & Councils. That list includes passports, medical directives or durable powers of attorney, health care proxies and revocable living wills."

Bank safe deposit boxes are only accessible during branch operating hours and the boxes are typically sealed when the bank receives a death notice. To open a sealed safe deposit box, estate representatives are required to provide court papers to the bank.

Items to store in safe deposit boxes might be:

- Property Deeds

- Savings Bonds

- Vehicle Titles

- Jewelry

- Household Inventory Photos

- Family Heirlooms

- Photo Negatives

RESOURCE LINKS

"Coping with the after effects of a disaster is difficult under any circumstance, but when vital records are lost, the trauma compounds. If you haven't done so already, take a few hours to organize your important documents and put them in a safe place. Even if you never experience a disaster, the peace of mind gained from organizing your records is well worth the few hours spent on this important task," advises USCG.

FEMA: Critical Documents and Valuable (PDF Online)

FDIC: What Documents to Keep Where (PDF Online)

CHECKLIST

Objective: To *gather and identify important papers, original documents, and make decisions on where to put them.*

☐ Research safe deposit boxes at your bank or in your community. Determine costs, hours of bank operation, and who has access to the box. Decide if this is a good solution for your documents.

☐ Research the cost of home fireproof and waterproof safes.

☐ Organize important papers into two groups: (1) original documents, papers and information that would be difficult or impossible to replace but that I wouldn't need immediate access to in the case of disaster or death and (2) important documents, papers and information I would need access to in the event of disaster or death.

☐ Consulting the Paper Timeline, eliminate unnecessary paper.

☐ Sort important papers and documents into appropriate files per the Paper Timeline.

TOMORROW

Creating a Mail Station

DAY 14: MAIL STATION

OBJECTIVE: TO CREATE A MAIL STATION

This is the last day we'll be dealing with paperwork!

But paper is a part of our everyday lives — and today's topic, mail, is one of the biggest paper clutter contributors.

Today we'll create a mail station that will effectively deal with daily mail and incoming paperwork as well some ideas on streamlining bill pay.

But first, a reminder of what you've accomplished in the home office so far...

CALENDAR

The office area is so important that we've split it up into 4 days as follows:

- **Day 11**: The Office
- **Day 12**: Creating a Filing System
- **Day 13**: Organizing Important Papers and Original Documents
- **Day 14**: Creating a Mail Station *(today)*

A MAIL STATION

INBOX

Designate a bin, a box, basket or drawer that can hold up to a week's worth of daily mail and paperwork that comes home (school, work, charitable, clubs, etc.). Deposit mail and paperwork immediately into the inbox, skipping counters, desktops, etc.

Have the inbox conveniently located where you will open mail, pay bills, calendar items and file paperwork.

Post a recycle bin near the inbox so as you bring in the daily mail, you can immediately recycle junk mail.

Schedule a **few minutes daily** or *at least weekly* to go through the inbox.

Open all the mail and distribute items to organizational systems you've created (bills to bill file, calendar items, correspondence, etc.).

MAIL TOOLS

Create a small bin, envelope, basket or tray that will contain items needed to process and answer mail (reply envelopes, letter opener, stamps, envelope moistener, pens, and so on).

PAYING BILLS

Create a bill file or folder that should be kept in your Action Files. This can be a single file which would hold all bills, a 5-pocket file organized by week of bill due date or a 31-day accordion file where due dates are organized by day of the month.

Determine a bill paying schedule (monthly, bimonthly, weekly, or immediately as your process mail).

Create a bill paying calendar: online, personal financial management software, or hardcopy.

Keep checkbook up to date.

CHECKLIST

Objective*: To organize daily mail and paperwork effectively.*

☐ Designate a mail and paperwork inbox.

☐ Place a recycling bin near the mail station.

☐ Create a small bin, tray or receptacle to contain items necessary to process mail (letter opener, stamps, etc.).

☐ Create a bill file in your Action Files.

☐ Determine an inbox processing schedule – daily is preferable, but at least weekly.

☐ Determine a bill paying schedule.

☐ Collect and sort all mail into 3 piles: action, bills, recycle.

☐ Take action on bills and paperwork

☐ Congratulations! You've now organized your entire home office. A place for everything, a system that will work, and the peace of knowing where things go!

TOMORROW

Master Bedroom

MAIL STATION INSPIRATIONS

AMW Design Studio, Pottery Barn, Real Simple, World Market, The Happy Housie

DAY 15: MASTER BEDROOM

OBJECTIVE: MASTER BEDROOM

The master bedroom is the most intimate and personal room in your home.

An oasis, a comfort zone, a classic retreat, and sweet dreams are all phrases that describe a master suite.

Or should.

Does that describe your master suite?

If you're like me, it depends on the day.

But it should be the goal!

However...

It might be the last room to get organized, the last to be tidied up, the last to get needed attention.

Why?

There are so many surfaces in the master bedroom. There's the bed, of course, and then there is *under the bed*, the night stands, the bureau, the trinkets, and so on.

And then... there are those pesky uncompleted or half-completed projects — whether that be laundry, a craft project or even work. Perhaps even a stack of books with your name on it. And too often, it can be yet another drop zone.

The last thing you see before closing your eyes on a busy day and the first in a new day... are those projects.

It's not conducive to tranquility or a great start to a new day.

We all deserve great starts and new days.

Sleep experts say our bedrooms need to be a haven and a sanctuary.

And while we know it's true, real life can get in the way. Crazy days, demanding schedules, and responsibilities can leave our rooms chaotic. Adding yet another layer of stress.

Let's get back to sweet dreams and organize our personal space, transforming it into a beautiful sanctuary.

Let's fill the bedroom with furniture that pleases the eye, linens that invite you to get comfortable and personal treasures that make you smile.

CALENDAR

The next three days...

- **Day 15**: Master Bedroom
- **Day 16**: Master Closet
- **Day 17**: Master Bath

SANCTUARY

Before the clutter elimination begins, take a few minutes and imagine what a master oasis or sanctuary might look like to you. What kinds of things help you relax? Make you smile? Do you read, watch TV... journal?

Get a picture in your mind of what that might look like, and pair back everything in your room that doesn't contribute to it.

Consider other possible locations for furniture items, even exercise equipment, that clutter your room.

You might want to read, "Perfect Sleep Bedtime Rituals" article at www.31daily.com for some inspiration.

ELIMINATE

Gather 3 boxes or bins and a couple of garbage bags.

1. Put Away Box – items that belong in other rooms

2. Donation Box – items you don't need but are in good condition

3. Storage Box – items you want to keep but not in your bedroom

Set a time limit, it seems less overwhelming that way. Say 15 minutes — maybe 20.

Fill the appropriate boxes and garbage bags. Be thorough and be quick. The more quickly you make these decisions, the easier it will be. **Begin with easy decisions and graduate to more difficult ones.**

Don't forget out of the way places — like under the bed, the bureau, the night stands — drawers — and any other storage areas you have in your bedroom. Set the boxes aside — even in the hallway.

GROUP

Group the items you are keeping in the room into piles of like items per location. All surfaces should be cleared as we'll be cleaning and vacuuming.

CLEAN

Once you've cleared out the room, strip the bedding and either launder it or plan to have it dry cleaned.

If weather permits, open windows and allow the room to air out as you work.

Clean and dust all surfaces and vacuum any upholstery, drapes or blinds.

Determine a weekly schedule that will allow you to keep your room as fresh and clean as it now is!

ORGANIZE AND BEAUTIFY

You have a clean slate. Recall that mind image you created at the beginning of this project? That beautiful, relaxing sanctuary?

It's time to create it!

For the items returning to your room, find functional yet beautiful storage. Especially for the small items.

Strategically light the areas that need it. If you like to read in bed, be sure to task light that area. If you have a favorite chair you like to sit and knit or read... be sure to light that area as well.

And finally, beautify your room. Add those personal treasures that make you smile at the end of each day and the beginning of the next.

Lastly... put some fresh flowers on your nightstand and or a piece of chocolate on your pillow. Reward yourself for a job well done!

CHECKLIST

Objective: *To create a personal haven in your master bedroom by eliminating everything that deters from it.*

- ☐ Clear all surfaces of the room, including under furniture, the bed and anything on the floor.

- ☐ Sort all items in the room and place in a put-away box, a donation box, a storage box or a garbage bag.

- ☐ Pile the things you are keeping in the room in another area and group into like items.

- ☐ Strip the bedding and either launder or schedule a dry-cleaning.

☐ Clean, dust and vacuum all surfaces, including upholstery, blinds, drapery, and furniture.

☐ Light your room appropriate to determined use.

☐ Organize items that come back into the room into attractive storage trays, bins, baskets, etc.

☐ Beautify the room and... indulge with a vase of fresh flowers on your nightstand or a piece of chocolate on your pillow.

☐ Immediately take care of your boxes.

TOMORROW

Master Closet

MASTER BEDROOM INSPIRATIONS

Traditional Home, Dear Lillie Blog, Zillow

DAY 16: MASTER CLOSET

OBJECTIVE: MASTER CLOSET

No matter the size, closets can quickly become organizational disasters. With an abundance of clothes and shoes, not to mention accessories, they can quickly become cluttered chaos without a storage system.

Even without a closet system, there are steps that can be taken to streamline closet organization.

With a simple step-by-step plan, you can have a functional closet and find what you need.

CALENDAR

The next three days...

- **Day 15**: Master Bedroom
- **Day 16**: Master Closet
- **Day 17**: Master Bath

5-STEP PLAN

STEP ONE: EMPTY THE CLOSET

Designate a staging area and empty your closet. This step is critical and in order to be effective, it's important to remove everything (hangers and all), leaving it completely empty.

If you have a collapsible or mobile clothes rack, this makes the job a lot easier to see exactly what you have. Having a partner makes this job a whole lot more fun.

STEP TWO: SORT

You will need:

A Put Away Box – for items that belong in other spaces

A Donation Box – for items that are wearable but no longer needed or wanted

Trash Bags – for items that are no longer wearable

Group items into specific categories and sort appropriately. If you are keeping the item, place it in a box or bin with like items (handbags, shoes, accessories, sweaters).

STEP THREE: ELIMINATE

This is one of the most difficult parts of organizing a closet. Deciding what to eliminate. As always, begin with the easy choices and graduate to the more difficult ones.

For instance, discard items that are unwearable, have holes, shoes that are have lost their mate and so on.

The idea is to eliminate down to a manageable amount.

If you have room, at this point, it's nice to separate out-of-season clothing if you can store it elsewhere. Large bins under the bed, high shelves fixed with storage containers are excellent ideas to store out-of-season clothing.

Related Articles Online:

"How to Store Seasonal Clothing":
http://www.hgtv.com/design/decorating/clean-and-organize/store-seasonal-clothing

"How to Switch Out Seasonal Clothing":
http://www.hgtv.com/design/decorating/clean-and-organize/how-to-switch-out-seasonal-clothing

Experts advise donating clothing not worn at least twice in a season, or that no longer fits, or that you don't love. One method, dubbed The Discardian Trick, is to turn all hangers the wrong way with the hook facing you. Once you wear an item, return it to the closet with the hanger hook facing the right way. Apparently, at the end of the season, it's easy to then discover which items you didn't wear. All hangers with the hook facing you.

Sometimes, clothing, however, can be an investment. Quality construction and fabrics can outlast many seasons. I like to buy simple and classic clothing that can be wardrobe staples for many seasons.

It all depends on your shopping and style personality.

For items you've designated to the elimination boxes, immediately remove them to another area so that you can concentrate on what you've decided to keep.

Return items from the Put-Away Box to their proper home before continuing.

STEP FOUR: ORGANIZE

Now that the unwanted items have been removed, it's time to concentrate on organization. Take a look at the keeper bins and clothing you will be returning to the closet.

It would be nice to have a custom closet organizational system where every item has a place. But if that dream is still in your future, you can organize your things by first grouping like items together and then find creative storage solutions to manage, especially, accessories.

Most home and organizational stores have innovative specialty storage features you can easily incorporate into your closet. The Container Store, Marshall's Home Goods, Home Depot, Target, Walmart and Amazon.com are easy places to shop.

Think vertical. Most closets have a tall headspace and is a perfect solution for out of season clothing or items rarely used. Don't neglect this important use of space.

Throw away wire hangers. Although they're convenient as dry cleaning items always return home on them, invest in some sturdy hangers and even padded hangers for delicate items. You'll be glad you did.

There are several ways to organize the clothes in your closet. Some prefer to organize by outfit, although this doesn't lend a pretty look to your closet and can be more difficult to mix-and-match pieces. Another way is to organize by color, which lends itself to a streamlined and organized look and allows you to know how many pieces you have in each color, avoiding duplication when shopping. And finally, most popular is to organize by type – all pants together, skirts, dresses, blouses, etc. Personally, I like a combination of color and type. But find a system that works best for you.

SIMPLE CLOSET ORGANIZATION IDEAS AT AMAZON.COM

STEP FIVE: CLEAN

You're almost done. Don't skip this important step.

Clean the closet itself. Wipe down the closet walls and vacuum or mop the floor.

Return clothing, accessories and storage solutions to your newly cleaned and organized master closet.

CHECKLIST

Objective: *To organize the master closet with 5 easy and simple steps.*

☐ Designate a staging area for closet contents.

☐ Empty the closet. (*Even the hangers*).

☐ Sort items and group by function.

☐ Eliminate items using either a "Put Away" Box, a Donation Box or a garbage bag.

☐ Return items to their proper home from the "Put Away" Box.

☐ Consider putting away seasonal clothing to help eliminate mass in the closet.

☐ Find simple yet functional storage for items like belts, ties, scarfs, handbags and so on.

☐ Clean the closet (walls, floors).

☐ Return items to the closet and organize as makes sense to you: by outfit, color, type — or a combination.

TOMORROW

Master Bath

MASTER CLOSET INSPIRATIONS

HGTV, Martha Stewart, Better Homes & Gardens

DAY 17: MASTER BATH

OBJECTIVE: MASTER BATH

"Our life is frittered
away by detail...
simplify, simplify."

~Henry David Thoreau

Next to the kitchen, the master bath is a daily use room that
can almost instantly become cluttered. With a messy
assortment of cosmetics, beauty items, products, hair dryers,
curling irons... and more... it can become a challenge. With a

few easy tricks and ideas, and in 3 easy steps, this room can be both functional and pleasant.

CALENDAR

The next three days...

- **Day 15**: Master Bedroom
- **Day 16**: Master Closet
- **Day 17**: Master Bath

3-STEP PLAN

As always: create a "Put Away" Box and a "Donation" Box, and grab several garbage bags.

STEP ONE: SORT AND CLEAN

Sort and eliminate expired products, unused items, and products with bulky packaging – and repackage into usable containers. Thoroughly clean and sanitize your bathroom, laundering bath mats, towels, and so on.

Start with the shower and keep only what you use daily, and then move to the cabinets and other areas. Thoroughly clean and sanitize your bathroom, laundering bath mats, towels, and so on.

Thoroughly clean and sanitize your bathroom, laundering bath mats, towels, and so on — eliminate sponges and loofahs because they are most likely supporting their own ecosystem.

STEP TWO: FIND USABLE STORAGE

Usable storage helps eliminate clutter by giving everything a home. Especially important in shared bathrooms. Products sitting on counters, bath ledges, windowsills, and other surfaces contributes to clutter, disorganization, and stress. The bathroom needs to function well.

Find innovative solutions like: back of the door racks, hanging organizers for the shower if you don't have built in shelves, drawer dividers for cosmetic and daily use items (toothbrushes, combs, razors, and so on) over-the-door-shoe caddies can double as holders for lotions, and other products. Be creative.

Easy Bathroom Storage Ideas:

- Container Store

- Crate & Barrel

- Walmart

- Amazon.com

STEP THREE: FUNCTION

This seems counterintuitive, but by adding specific pieces of furniture to your bathroom, you'll actually increase your space capacity.

Ideas would be tall, vertical cabinets for more storage, towel cabinets, or bath racks.

Melanie Gomez in Smart, *Space Saving Bathroom Storage* says:

Drawers: "Sharing is important in any relationship, but not when it comes to the bathroom. Case in point: the sharp-elbowed nudges caused by an unorganized vanity. The solution is to divvy up surfaces and compartments.

Under Sink: "Fit central cabinets with roll-out trays, like ones you'd see in a kitchen cabinet."

Cabinets: "Keep to Yourself — Side cabinets, like the vanity's countertops, should be divided as well. Keep his shaving stuff in a portable basket and store towels (and maybe some of her stuff) on the spare shelves in his cabinet."

CHECKLIST

Objective: With a simple 3-Step plan, this important room can function efficiently.

☐ Remove all items that belong in other rooms.

☐ Remove all items from drawers, cabinets, and under the sink to sort.

☐ Discard all expired items, items that are broken, in poor condition or that are no longer used.

☐ Thoroughly clean and sanitize the bathroom, wipe out drawers and cabinets.

☐ Create functional storage, grouping items by use: daily, weekly/monthly and rarely. Daily use items need to be readily accessible, weekly or more use items in drawers and rarely used items are candidates for harder to reach storage.

☐ Purchase items necessary to keep the bathroom clean; shower squeegees, and so on. Discard any used loofas, sponges, etc. They can support their own ecosystem.

☐ Put away items belonging in other rooms.

TOMORROW

Kid's and Guest Rooms

MASTER BATH INSPIRATIONS

Pottery Barn, Decorpad.com, Good Housekeeping,
cocondedecoration.com

DAY 18: KIDS AND GUEST BEDROOMS

OBJECTIVE: KIDS AND GUEST BEDROOMS

Children's rooms can be one of the most challenging rooms to not only organize... but keep that way. And much depends on the child's age. Some are natural-born organizers, others are direct opposites. Only you can determine the best path toward an organized room keeping in clear view each child's individual needs and disposition.

However, one thing I learned with my now teenager, is to make it fun. Putting away toys, hanging up clothes, tidying up their room — all of it. Make it a game, and reward often. Don't allow unclean rooms and disorganized closets and toys become stumbling blocks in your relationship with your child.

That being said, even at a young age, basic organization can and should be taught. How well it takes, depends on the child. Organizational tools will follow them throughout life and it is important. But more important is their relationship with you.

AGE APPROPRIATE ORGANIZATION

TODDLERS (2-4)

"Generally, toddlers enjoy being helpful and won't see cleaning as work unless you make it sound like work," says Donna Smallin, author of *Cleaning Plain & Simple*, "Keep an upbeat attitude, and make sure you give little ones lots of praise."

- Make it fun

- Make it a game

- Cleaning is a cooperative project

- Store like items together

AGES 5-8

"Children in this age range love to get creative, and if you give them a challenge they'll thrive on rising to the occasion," says Tara Aronson, author of *Mrs. Clean Jeans' Housekeeping with Kids.* "They can also start handling a lot more responsibility."

- Make it accessible

- Give them responsibility

- Establish zones

- Establish limits for how much stuff can be kept in the room

- Get creative with storage

AGES 9-12

"This is the age where you need to give your children even more responsibility for their possessions, as well as their choices," says professional organizer and TV host Peter Walsh. "More and more, they're making decisions about what they spend their money on, what's valuable to them and what can be given to charity or sold."

- Teach organizational life skills

- Let them help establish their own routines

- Let them help choose organizational methods

- Don't nag

For more specific ideas on age appropriate organizational ideas, read "Get Your Kids Organized at All Ages."

A couple of my favorite books on child rearing with age appropriate responsibilities are:

BONDING WITH YOUR CHILD THROUGH BOUNDARIES

Author: June Hunt

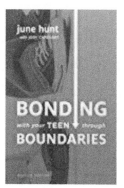

BONDING WITH YOUR TEEN THROUGH BOUNDARIES (REVISED EDITION)

Author: June Hunt

A TOY LIBRARY

As with all the other rooms in your home, elimination will be key to an organized life for your kids. Chaos can be better controlled by setting some limits and boundaries.

One of the most effective ways of keeping toys organized, is to create a toy library. My mom taught me this trick... and it worked really well for us.

First, sort through all their toys, eliminating broken toys, those that are missing parts and can't be played with because of it, or toys they've outgrown or aren't interested in. Remove them to either a trash bag or donation box.

Finally, box up half of them and put them away where they cannot be seen. Don't store the box in a location that can be seen.

In a few months, return the toys you've left out (unless they are a favorite, everyday toy) and check out the "new" toys that have been in storage. Do this every few months, eliminating toys as they break or as a child loses interest or outgrows.

CONSIDER ROOM NEEDS

Kids

Organize kid's rooms around floor play space, keeping safety in mind always. Organize also from the bottom of the room to the top, keeping their height in mind, their daily use items, making it as simple as possible to put things away.

Teens

Teen room needs change from when they are younger. Play space becomes study space. Optimize the study area by providing a desk that fits them, and drawers to keep their study tools organized. Shelves become very important, labeled containers to corral their stuff and peg boards, memo boards or bulletin boards are great places for reminders, events, and mementos.

Guest Rooms

The focus in this room is a comfortable bed and cozy linens. Be sure to include a clock in the room, some reading materials, ample task lighting, and a luggage rack is very helpful. Before guests arrive, stock the room with freshly laundered towels, a snack basket of items you know they'd like, some toiletries and bottles of water — and a small, fresh flower arrangement is always welcome!

CHECKLIST

Objective: To organize kid's rooms by teaching age-appropriate organizational behavior and/or outfit a guest room.

- ☐ Create a Put-Away Box, a Donation Box and gather several trash bags.

- ☐ Remove all items that belong in other rooms and deposit into the Put Away Box.

- ☐ With the child's help (age appropriate), quickly sort through all items in the room and determine whether to keep, toss or donate.

- ☐ Determine if there is another room to store toys.

- ☐ For the items that will be kept in the room, create functional storage bins, baskets, etc., and label everything!

- ☐ Clean the room thoroughly and launder all bed linens. Vacuum all corners and under the bed.

☐ If necessary, rearrange furniture to either create more floor space, study space or flow space for guests.

☐ Repeat steps with the closet, putting away items that belong in other rooms, eliminating clothing that is either worn out or no longer fits. Create easy-access functional storage for items stored in the closet.

TOMORROW

Family Bathrooms

KIDS AND GUEST ROOM INSPIRATIONS

quintessenceblog.com, House Beautiful, Pottery Barn Teen, Centsational Girl

HGTV, Good Housekeeping

DAY 19: FAMILY BATHROOMS

OBJECTIVE: FAMILY BATHROOMS

Family bathrooms can be notorious sources of strife, especially among female occupants or wide age ranges or even gender. And while organization can't alleviate all of it, it can profoundly help!

Here are some easy ways to implement personal storage, organizational structure, and tricks for common use items that will go a long way toward conciliation without last minute scrambles for curling irons, toothbrushes and more!

CREATE STORAGE ELSEWHERE

Find storage elsewhere for bulky items, excess products, medicinal items, and first aid kits. When the bathroom is in use, these items will still be available.

Better Homes & Gardens

PERSONAL CADDY

Personal caddies, complete with all the items necessary to get ready in the morning, alleviates a lot of tension as each occupant has their own supplies. This one, from Pottery Barn, is also great for dorm rooms or sleep-overs.

Pottery Barn Teen

IMPLEMENT STORAGE FOR HIGH USE ITEMS

Create storage for high use items like towels, toiletries (cotton balls, cue tips), toilet paper and more. Consider installing vertical storage, like the area above the toilet, or other wall space to maximize storage for common use items. Using counter-top acrylic see-through containers for cotton balls, cue tips and other items frees up drawer space, provides easy access, and is easy to keep track of inventory.

CHECKLIST

Objective: To organize a family bathroom that functions well for multiple family members.

☐ Create a Put-Away Box, a Donation Box and gather several trash bags.

☐ Remove all items that belong in other rooms and deposit into the Put Away Box.

☐ Sort through all the bathroom products and discard any expired items.

☐ Separate out multiples of a product, bulky excess products and first aid kits to locate elsewhere.

☐ Create personal caddies for each family member and organize products in them. Locate these caddies in their bedroom.

☐ Create storage where appropriate; vertical, wall space, etc., to store high use and common use items. Create store for small like items (plastic lidded bins, baskets, etc.)

☐ Clean and sanitize all fixtures, drawers, and cabinets.

☐ Restock the newly cleaned and organized bathroom.

TOMORROW

Bonus Rooms and Areas

FAMILY BATHROOM INSPIRATIONS

Martha Stewart, Southern Living, Real Simple

DAY 20: BONUS ROOMS

OBJECTIVE: BONUS ROOMS

The beauty of a bonus room is just that... they are a **bonus**.

While some homes are designed with that extra space —
others are not. But that isn't as limiting as one might expect.

Bonus rooms can be created out of unusual spaces. They can
be carved from awkward nooks, unused bedrooms, portions
of other rooms, lofts, landings, basements, or even covered
porches. They can be carriage houses or sheds or even attics.

And they can be used for anything your heart desires;
playrooms, media rooms, music rooms, theaters, man caves,
craft rooms, game rooms, rec rooms. The only limitation is
your creativity.

I love these rooms. Multi-use spaces that can grow and change as your family does.

Organizing these rooms are completely dependent on their use.

But a few rules still apply. And those are the same tools and mindset we've employed through now 20 days of organizing the home.

Controlling clutter by eliminating excess, grouping items in categories that make sense, creating functional storage – which importantly results in giving everything a home.

Let's get to work on multi-use bonus rooms, which often comes with multi-use clutter, and give those odds and ends a home.

CREATE ZONES

Bonus rooms are generally open spaces that need to serve several functions.

Create zones for the various activities that will take place in the room. Using space planning, create areas for play, gaming, TV watching, studying, crafting, reading... and anything else planned for this room.

Be sure to include comfortable seating as this room is a fun room and will attract friends and family.

CREATE STORAGE

For high-use items with many parts — clear, lidded and labeled plastic storage works wonders like these from the Container Store.

GOING UP NOT OUT!

Use vertical space whenever available to help maximize square footage. Extra tall bookshelves work wonders with books, games and more.

Country Living

CHECKLIST

Objective: *To organize a family fun room.*

☐ Determine how you want to use this room.

☐ Take a blank piece of paper and draw a floor plan, roughly penciling activity zones for the room.

☐ With plan in place, remove everything from the room that doesn't fit your plan.

☐ Create structure, likes shelves, to store organized items.

☐ Create functional use storage for small items, like toys, craft supplies and so on. Be sure to clearly label each bin.

☐ Sort through items in the room and eliminate anything that is either broken or unwanted and either discard immediately or put in a donation box.

☐ Group like items together by category. For toys, plastic bins labeled; farm toys, police, art supplies, hot wheels *(can you tell I had a little boy?)* are easy to keep organized.

☐ Return newly organized items, including bins, into their organizational zones.

☐ Create a comfortable seating area.

TOMORROW

Laundry Room

BONUS ROOM INSPIRATIONS

Stonehand.com, Houseplans.co, Better Homes & Gardens, abowlfulloflemons.net

DAY 21: LAUNDRY ROOM

OBJECTIVE: LAUNDRY ROOM

Laundry Rooms can become catchall rooms for everything that walks in the door. But these "work rooms" don't have to be the forgotten room, they can be as clean and organized as the rest of our house. Making them a pleasure to "work" in.

But as in all areas of the home, there are a lot of pieces that add to messy clutter if not organized and streamlined.

Let's walk through some steps to help streamline laundry room functionality. Tomorrow we'll compile of list of recommended supplies every laundry room should have.

1. HAMPERS

Before you even begin to organize your laundry room, be sure that every bedroom has a laundry hamper or basket. When it's time for laundry, the process is much easier than crawling around on hands and knees picking up dirty socks.

2. DETERMINE USE

Of course, laundry rooms are for laundering and cleaning clothes. But depending on its size, it can be used for more. For instance, I've had laundry rooms that had areas for a sewing machine as well as a dry-goods larder. I've also had laundry rooms that were merely a hall closet. Maximize and utilize every square inch of what you have.

3. ELEMENTS

By adding space-saving elements to laundry rooms, you can increase their efficiency. All laundry rooms need some kind of shelving, either cabinets, simple wire racks above the washer and dryer or freestanding wire units. It's also nice to include an ironing board, a drying rack (free-standing, an inexpensive retractable line or a drying bar) and storage containers, a must.

Basic Needs for a Laundry Room

- Shelving

- Ironing Board

- Drying Rack

- Folding Table

- 3-Bin Laundry Sorter for Dirty Clothes (lights, darks, and towels)

- Catchall Bin for loose change, buttons or anything else found in pockets

- Folding Surface

- Laundry Basket for Clean Clothes/Towels Transport

4. CREATE BEAUTY

Put something of beauty in this room, or closet. Something that brightens your day and make this room feel like it's part of your larger home. Whether that be a print hung on a wall, beautiful basket storage containers or printed containers with a pleasing design. Buy something new for your room that will make it seem fresh.

SETTING UP THE LAUNDRY ROOM

Whether your laundry room is a tiny closet or a spacious basement, organization is key. These 10 tips will help you make the most of the space you have.

1. Arrange products and supplies according to how you use them. Anything you regularly need should be within easy reach; place extras and incidentals on a high shelf or another out-of-the-way spot.

2. Decant detergents from large boxes and jugs into smaller containers or soap boxes; refill as needed.

3. Store small supplies in boxes or bins: Place stain-removal products in one, sewing materials in another, and sponges in a third. Have rags on hand for spills.

4. Sort whites, colors, delicates, and heavily soiled items in bins or rolling carts.

5. If you don't have room for a folding table, affix a fold-down shelf to the wall.

6. Keep a drying rack handy for drip-dry items.

7. Attach an ironing-board hanger to the wall so the board and iron are secure and out of the way but easily accessible.

8. Install a rod in the laundry room on which to hang clothes as you iron; or install a hook over the top of a door to serve the same purpose.

9. Keep clothes hangers and mesh bags for delicates with your cleaning supplies or in a nearby cabinet.

10. Use free space in the laundry room to store gift wrap, ribbon, basic tools, and pet supplies.

Source: Martha Stewart – Organizing the Laundry Room

CLOTHING

FOLDING

- When tumble-dried clothes are dry—preferably when they are still warm—hang them up or smooth them out and fold them right away. Avoid having them sit and cool in a crumpled state.

- Clothes that should be folded include: T-shirts, sweaters, jeans, sweats—basically anything knit or stretchy.

- Folded clothes are easier to transport.

HANGING

- Hanging certain garments as they emerge from the dryer can save on ironing time.

- Clothes that should be hung include: creased or pleated items, button-down shirts, khakis—anything that wrinkles easily.

- Wooden hangers with a rod work for most hangable items. Choose padded hangers for fragile items, and hangers with rubber clips for skirts (metal clips might dent the fabric).

Source: Real Simple – Setting Up an Efficient Laundry Room

CHECKLIST

Objective: *To increase efficiency by organizing and utilizing every square foot of the laundry room.*

☐ Clear the room of all products and sort, discarding any expired items.

☐ Create a Put Away Box and immediately return items that don't belong in the laundry room to their home.

☐ Sort products in the laundry room by use and contain them in baskets, bins or containers.

☐ Install functional storage; shelves, racks, ironing board, dirty laundry bins and so on.

☐ Clean and sanitize all surfaces in the room, including the washing machine and dryer.

☐ Hide supplies as much as possible to rid the room of messy clutter. Keep out only the products you need for laundry.

☐ Create small bins and stock necessary supplies for the following kits: minor sewing repair and stain removal.

☐ Put something pretty in the room that motivates and inspires.

TOMORROW

Laundry Supplies

LAUNDRY ROOM INSPIRATIONS

DAY 22: LAUNDRY SUPPLIES

OBJECTIVE: LAUNDRY SUPPLIES CHECKLIST

Yesterday we organized the laundry room.

Today, we will revisit the laundry room and the supplies we stock. It doesn't take dozens and dozens of bottles, potions, and powders to have the necessary ingredients to remove stains, launder clothes, and sanitize.

By pairing down to supplies that are actually needed and by decanting bulky packaging into streamlined clear and labeled containers, laundry rooms become more efficient and easier to work in. It's all about simplification.

Begin with this basic laundry supply list.

LAUNDRY SUPPLY CHECKLIST

Liquid Detergent

Baking soda – a gentle detergent booster and natural fabric softener

Borax – a detergent booster and aid that is gentle, cleans, deodorizes, softens water, and helps get rid of stains

Chlorine bleach – a must have for disinfecting and whites.

Color Safe bleach – safe for colored fabrics, added to presoak or wash water with detergent

Washing soda or sodium carbonate – presoaking or as a detergent builder

White vinegar – softens water, whitens fabrics

Fabric Softener – comes in dryer sheets, liquid form

Stain Remover – commercial variety or create your own DIY Stain Removal Kit

Download and Print Laundry Supply List: http://www.31daily.com/wp-content/uploads/2016/09/31Daily-Easy-Steps-to-an-Organized-Life-Laundry-Supply-List.pdf

STAIN REMOVAL KIT

Stock these items to effectively and naturally remove stains: **cornstarch**, to absorb fresh grease stains; oil solvents, or dry-cleaning fluids, for greasy residue; combination solvents and a mild, **clear dishwashing liquid** for all-purpose stain removal; **natural bleaching agents** (lemon juice and white vinegar); **glycerin**, for ballpoint ink; and eyedroppers and cotton swabs, for easy application.

> Download and Print Martha Stewart Stain Removal Chart: http://www.31daily.com/wp-content/uploads/2016/09/stain_removal_basics.pdf

BRIGHTENING WHITES WITHOUT BLEACH

Whites can also be lightened with 1/2 cup of borax or white vinegar mixed into one gallon of water during the wash cycle. For an extra brightening boost, hang laundry in the sun for natural bleaching.

DIY FABRIC SOFTENER

Residues from fabric softeners and their fragrances can aggravate allergies and sensitivities, and leave buildup on moisture sensors or lint screens, blocking air flow.

For a DIY fabric softener, add between 1/4 cup and 1 cup white vinegar to the final rinse cycle (never mix vinegar and chlorine bleach).

DIY LIQUID LAUNDRY DETERGENT

Dr. Bronner's is one of the most popular liquid Castile soaps available. Most markets stock this, but you can also get it at Amazon.com

2 1/4 cups liquid castile soap
1/4 cup white distilled vinegar
1 tablespoon glycerin
3/4 cup water

Combine all ingredients into a plastic container or squirt bottle. Shake once or twice before adding to the wash. To use, add 1/4 cup per average load; 1/2 cup for extra-large or heavily soiled loads.

DIY POWDER LAUNDRY DETERGENT

2 cups finely grated bar soap – Mrs. Meyers works great *(do not use the box grater from the kitchen!)*
1 cup borax
1 cup washing soda

Mix well and store in an airtight container.

Use 2 tablespoons per load.

WASHER AND DRYER MAINTENANCE

To keep the all-important washer and dryer working efficiently, it must be regularly maintained. Weekly, wipe the washer's interior with a clean, damp cloth, then run a short hot wash cycle with detergent; rinse the empty machine with a plain water cycle. At least once a month, disinfect with chlorine bleach solution on a short hot wash cycle. To prevent the dryer from overheating, clean the screen or filter after every use, and remove accumulated lint from behind the dryer.

CHECKLIST

Objective: to stock and restock necessary laundry supplies

☐ Print the Stain Removal Chart above and post in the laundry.

☐ Print the Laundry Supply Checklist to have as a resource.

☐ Inventory current supplies and add to what you currently have if necessary.

☐ Create a stain remover kit and contain items in clear, labeled storage.

TOMORROW

Linen Closet

DAY 23: LINEN CLOSET

OBJECTIVE: LINEN CLOSET

Linen closets have a way of becoming unruly, towering piles of towels, bedsheets and a myriad collection of odds and ends. It's one of the areas we always intend to correct, fix, organize... but sometimes those intentions have a way of staying in the future.

Today, we'll tackle the linen closet — and it's easier than you might think!

With a few guidelines, and tricks, and inspirational photos, you'll be opening your linen closet door to all your guests — a closet you'll be proud of.

FRESH LINENS

Airing Out

Give linens their space. "Air flow is important to the safe storage of most textiles," says Jonathan Scheer, president of J. Scheer & Co., a New York textile-preservation firm. "If they're stuffed into the back of a closet, the fibers retain more moisture, which attracts mold and mildew, which can be permanently damaging. You should take them out and air them every three months."

"You can chase away mustiness with an open container of baking soda, activated charcoal, or calcium carbonate," says Cheryl Mendelson, author of Home Comforts: The Art & Science of Keeping House ($22, Scribner, amazon.com).

Real Simple magazine suggests, "To enhance the aroma of your linens, place in the back of the closet sachet bags of pine, cedar, vanilla, or fresh lavender wrapped in cheesecloth and tied with a ribbon. You can also hang a fabric-softener strip on the door or use scented drawer liners, which are sold by the Container Store ($15 for four 18-by-24-inch sheets, containerstore.com) and other places."

SPACE

The ideal linen closet would be spacious enough to house all needed items, have adjustable shelves, and be at a 12 to 15-inch rise, perfect for short stacks of laundry.

If that doesn't describe your space, you can customize it with shelf dividers, baskets, plastic bins, and plastic-covered-wire shelving, all of which can be found at Ikea, ClosetMaid, the Container Store, and other organizing specialists. You can also adapt the closet by removing the bottom shelves and installing a counter three feet from the floor and placing beneath it rolling drawer units, pullout shelves, or laundry baskets. Be creative with the space you have and utilize every inch.

Label everything so that's it's easily identified.

FOLDING

TOWELS

Properly folded towels will keep your linen closet organized.

Bath towels should be folded in thirds, lengthwise, and then in half, and in half again.

FITTED SHEETS

Did you know that Google says 27,000 people a month search for "how to fold a fitted sheet?"

Here are 3 easy steps from Women's Day magazine.

Step 1: Tuck the corners from one side of the fitted sheet (yes, all fitted sheets have corners, despite how tricky they are to find) into the corners on the opposite side, point to point. Repeat with the other set of corners. By now, your fitted sheet should more closely resemble a flat sheet, just a little bunchier.

Step 2: Much like step 1, we're back to tucking in corners. This time, tuck one set of corners into the opposite set of corners. Less bunchy now, right?

Step 3: Fold in the two elastic sides to create straight edges. Then, you can go ahead and fold as you would a flat sheet. And voila: that neat square you never thought was possible. It took Clinton about 60 seconds to do it in the video above, which means that with a little practice, you can do it in way less time, since you won't be explaining the process to eager students.

CHECKLIST

Objective*: to freshen up and reorganize the linen closet so everything is easy to find and accessible.*

- ☐ Remove all items from the linen closet and sort by bedding for each bedroom, towels for each bathroom and table cloths, runners and table napkins.

- ☐ From the sorts, divide out seasonal items and special occasion items from everyday use.

- ☐ Return any items that belong in other rooms immediately.

- ☐ Wipe out the shelves, walls and doors of the linen closet.

- ☐ For bulky items, store in a plastic container, zippered bag or pillowcase to keep them dust free and locate on a top shelf.

- ☐ Next store out of season or special occasion linens also on a top shelf. If possible, store in zippered bag to keep free of dust.

- ☐ Eliminate any linens that are overly worn or are missing pieces if you have other sets in good condition (like bedsheets).

- ☐ Refold all towels and bedsheet sets that will remain.

☐ Locate towels and bedsheets at eye level.

☐ Locate occasional use items in the back or the top of the closet.

☐ For supplies kept in the linen closet, create functional storage to corral small, like items.

TOMORROW

Garage

LINEN CLOSET INSPIRATIONS

Better Homes & Gardens, Country Living

DAY 24: GARAGE

OBJECTIVE: GARAGE

Professional organizers estimate that only 30% of people are able to park their car in their garage.

Why?

Stuff.

Too much, for too long, with little elimination.

If you're like me, I'm not a fan of climbing into a freezing cold car in the winter, or a hot car in the summer. I like to park in the garage. It's safer, it's better for the investment of your vehicle, and more convenient when company visits.

While this is admittedly a big job and one that is much easier with a partner... it's doable. You just have to have a plan. An elimination plan... and a floor plan.

You can do this! And the reward of an organized and functioning garage for the whole family is well worth the effort.

BEST GARAGE ORGANIZATION TIPS

Label every container – most important tip.
Keep everything off the floor as much as possible.
Consider renting a storage unit for seasonal items.
Have a lined trash/recycle can in the garage for quick car cleaning.

EQUIPMENT EVERY GARAGE NEEDS

A Fire Extinguisher
A locked storage cabinet to store chemicals and fertilizers

WHAT NOT TO STORE IN THE GARAGE

Paint – extreme temperatures can ruin the paint.
Propane – a spark can ignite the propane – best to store outdoors.

Paper Plates, Napkins, etc. – paper goods are notorious for attracting bugs. Store indoors.

Pet Food – pet food attracts critters. Store in a sealed container outdoors.

Valuables – safety

Temperature Sensitive Heirlooms – paintings, photographs, important documents, delicate clothing (like wedding dresses)

CHECKLIST

Objective: to eliminate unwanted and unneeded items, to organize what's left, resulting in a functioning garage.

☐ **Lay out 3** tarps or boxes labeled: keep, donate, and toss and create distinct, separate areas.

☐ **Quickly sort through garage items** and locate either in the keep, donate or toss areas. In the discard pile, should be anything that is outgrown (like toys), broken beyond repair or that you haven't used in a couple of years.

☐ **Bag the discards and box the donation** piles. Locate them outside the garage and have a plan on when they will be either picked up by your garbage/recycle service, taken to the dump or donation center. Do this as quickly as possible. The longer they sit, the more likely they will find their way back into the garage.

☐ **Items to be kept:** sort into categories like sports equipment, automobile, hand tools, and so on. Box and label or ***better yet***, put in labeled clear, lidded plastic containers.

☐ **Draft a floor plan:** Roughly sketch the outline of the garage noting windows, doors, etc. along with dimensions. Add this to your household files.

☐ **Assign homes to everything** that will remain in the garage: lawn tools and fertilizers should be kept together, large equipment like lawn mowers, etc. in out of the way corners, frequent use items like scooters, bikes near the garage door and seasonal items in hardest to reach areas. Consider

☐ **Create a plan for storage:** Use vertical shelves to maximize space for plastic container storage, vertical systems that can be mounted to the wall, peg boards or hooks for the walls, ball bins for sports equipment, and overhead storage racks – perfect for long flat items you don't use every day *(kayaks come to mind)*.

☐ **Sweep out the garage** floor and walls and all its corners.

☐ **Mount or install storage racks,** systems, and so on and fill according to your floor plan.

☐ **Park your car** in the garage — and get takeout! You deserve it — job well done!

TOMORROW

Organize Photographs

GARAGE INSPIRATIONS

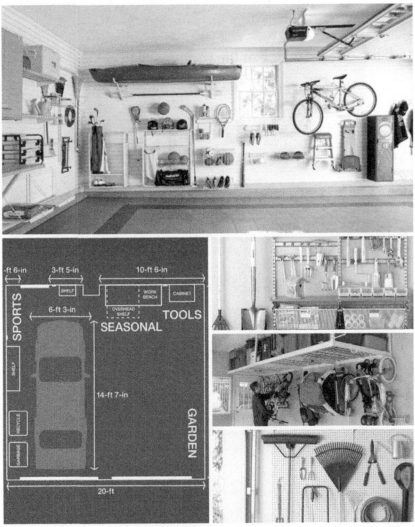

This Old House, Lowes, Container Store, Amazon, Good Housekeeping

DAY 25: PHOTOGRAPHS

OBJECTIVE: PHOTOGRAPHS

I have a staggering number for you.

Did you know that people worldwide take photos every 2 minutes? Per year — 657 billion photos according to Mary Meeker's Internet Trends Report. In 2015, she reports 3.5 million photos shared on social media, daily.

A lot of numbers to tell you something you already know. We take a lot of photos. And a lot of them sit on our devices for lack of knowing what to do with them.

How to manage and organize those photos are the topic today.

MONTHLY DIGITAL DOWNLOADS

Step 1: Storage

Decide how you want to store digital photos.

The Guardian advises, "The best option for individuals is an external hard drive, connected to your PC via a USB or Thunderbolt port. Powered USB 3 drives are big, fast, reasonably priced, and generally reliable." It also recommends that depending on the size of your photo archive, a 3TB size drive is best but anything between 2TB and 5TB. And most importantly, decide if you want to backup the media files on an additional external drive or an online cloud.

For more specific information and recommendations, read the article in The Guardian: https://www.theguardian.com/technology/askjack/2016/jun/23/whats-the-best-way-to-organise-and-store-my-digital-photos.

Step 2: Make Folders.

Make a single folder labeled "Pictures." Within that folder, you'll have sub-folders. Most import software will automatically create folders by year and month. These specifications can be changed in the settings if desire.

Decide whether you want to organize photos chronologically by year and month, or by theme and event. My preference is a hybrid on the two – I always import by year and then by month. But I also add tags to define events, themes, etc.

Step 3: Download

Once a month at the minimum, download all photos from your camera or phone to a computer desktop photo management program like iPhoto for Mac, Photo App for Windows 10 or older Windows versions – Windows Live Photo Gallery.

Step 4: Review

Import the photos and review. Immediately delete images that are out of focus or duplicates of the same scene.

Step 5: Back Up.

After each batch of uploaded photos, back up to either the backup external drive or a cloud service.

"The best backup is still a printed photo," says Cathi Nelson, founder of the Association of Personal Photo Organizers. But many experts say don't bother with a home printer — supplies are expensive and the quality rarely good. Instead, use an online service or a store kiosk. Nelson suggests trying a few stores to see which one churns out the best prints. And don't discount the small, independent shops. "Your local photo lab wants your business so is usually a great source of help and info," Nelson says.

ORGANIZE PRINT PHOTOS

The easiest first step in organizing print photos is to first gather them to one location.

Purchase a photo storage box or boxes, depending on your volume. Be sure these are specifically designed archival photo boxes. Amazon.com has some as does the Container Store.

Secondarily, as time permits and part of a longer-term project, purchase archival albums to store special photos in with slide-in sleeves.

Step 1: Organization

Create organizational dividers. Similar to digital photos, organize into broad categories or time frames.

Step 2: Sort

Sort printed photos and notate on the back of each with an acid-free, photo-safe pencil or pen any relevant information, dates, locations, people in the photos and so on.

Step 3: Eliminate

One of the hardest parts is eliminating photos. Begin eliminating easy choices; like bad exposures, or blurry shots.

As you come across favorites, set them aside to put into photo albums you already have or create a gallery wall in your home.

Step 4: Negatives and Slides

Negatives are best stored flat, in specifically designed acid free sleeves. You can find these on Amazon.com. Many experts advise to store them in a safe place like a safe deposit box or fire and waterproof safe.

Slides are also easily stored in archival sleeves for binders. You can also find these at Amazon.com.

Step 5: Label

Label everything possible. It will save you mountains of work in the years to come.

PROTECT PHOTOS

To protect your precious photos, keep these points in mind from Better Homes and Gardens.

- Temperature, humidity, and light affect photos. Stash stored photos and photo albums away from sunlight in a cool, dry area.

- Hang framed photos on a wall that won't get the direct sunlight, which fades photos quickly. Or use blinds and draperies to control the light.

- Avoid storing photos in basements or attics, where temperatures and humidity fluctuate.

- Oils on your fingers degrade photos and negatives, so handle them by the edges only. For additional protection, wear clean white cotton gloves.

- Paper clips, rubber bands, glue, and tape shouldn't come in contact with photos, unless specifically designed as safe for photos.

- Plastic pages, bags, and boxes that aren't acid-free might release harmful vapors that permanently damage photos. These plastic products are considered safe: polypropylene, polyethylene, Mylar, Tyvek, and cellulose triacetate. Before you buy, check labels on photo boxes, mats, and albums to make sure they're acid-free and photo-safe.

- Always frame photos using acid-free matting materials.

- Keep photos away from wood, plywood, chipboard, rubber cement, animal glue, shellac, contact cement, polyvinyl chloride (PVC), pressure-sensitive tape, and porous marking pens.

- Adhesives might chemically interact with images and ruin the photos if you try to remove them from an album at a later date. Use only specially made **acid-free glue sticks, markers, and corners** on your photos. (Available from *exposuresonline.com, archivalmethods.com, orarchivalusa.com.*)

- **Never** use so-called magnetic photo albums that have damaging glues on the photo pages.

CHECKLIST

Objective: to create a photo archive, schedule a monthly download and begin a print photo archive.

- ☐ **Begin with digital photos.** Download all photos onto chosen system; external drive, hard drive, etc.

- ☐ **Organize digital photos** by chosen organizational strategy – chronological or by theme/event — or a combination.

- ☐ **Review** photos and eliminate easy choices like; blurry, duplicate, etc.

- ☐ **Backup photos.**

- ☐ **Print Photos:** Create or purchase archival photo storage boxes or binders and label tabs or cards with broad dates and categories. These can be sub-divided at later dates.

- ☐ **Sort Prints:** as you sort, eliminate easy choices like blurry, overexposed or duplicates (unless you want to give it to a family member). Set aside favorite photos to either place in an existing album or frame.

☐ **Organize Negatives and Slides:** In the same way, organize negatives and slides into broad categories or dates. Store in specifically designed sleeves.

☐ **Storage.** Determine location to store binders or photo boxes in a temperature controlled environment.

TOMORROW

Books and Magazines

DAY 26: BOOKS & MAGAZINES

OBJECTIVE: BOOKS AND MAGAZINES

A new study conducted by Pew Research early in September 2016 reports:

"Americans today have an enormous variety of content available to them at any time of day, and this material is available in a number of formats and through a range of digitally connected devices. Yet even as the number of ways people spend their time has expanded, a Pew Research Center survey finds that the share of Americans who have read a book in the last 12 months (73%) has remained largely unchanged since 2012. And when people reach for a book, it is much more likely to be a traditional print book than a digital product."

What about young households? With social media connectivity, one might think millennial homes wouldn't be as cluttered with books and magazines as would, say, a baby boomer home. Think again.

"If you imagine millennials are just young people entranced by their cellphones or tablet computers, you might want to think again. According to a new study, 92% of college students would rather do their reading the old-fashioned way, with pages and not pixels" (LA Times).

The question then remains... what to do with the inevitable collection.

Here are a few suggestions. Let's begin with magazines.

MAGAZINES

STEP 1: ELIMINATE

It has to begin with elimination. It's hard, I know. When I donated all my Martha Stewart magazines from the beginning of time to the library, it wasn't a pleasant experience. But it had to be done. We were facing a multi-state move and I had boxes of magazines I dearly loved. Parting was not sweet but it was the right decision. I consoled myself with the idea that most of the content I loved would be available on the internet. And it was, and is. If I have a need to go back and look at particular issues, large libraries keep amazing periodical archives. It can be done.

The first step is to set aside magazine issues you love and are not willing to part with. Stack them up. See what you've got. And then eliminate the rest. Libraries are great places to donate past issues.

I'm not fond of the 1 in, 1 out theory of organization, simply because sometimes it isn't that arbitrary. However, I've settled for this: I have subscriptions to cooking and home decor magazines. They're inspirational and informative. But I only keep the issues seasonally. And then I either recycle or donate or pass along to a friend. I have a specific location for those issues in my meal planning area.

I also keep Thanksgiving and Christmas issues I particularly liked. And I have a bin for those.

STEP 2: KNOW YOUR LIMITS

Knowing your storage limit helps make informed decisions about what to keep.

STEP 3: STORAGE

The magazines you are keeping, organize by title, and then year, and then month. Create a dedicated storage area and container for these issues. Magazine holders work great, as do some baskets designed for the purpose.

BOOKS

If you love books as much as we do, this is difficult. We're the ones always shopping at the library sales, perusing new release titles and timeless classics. And our growing collection shows our love of the medium.

However, as it all things, there is a balance. Again, knowing what your storage limits are, helps make the decision a bit easier.

My husband and I have moved many times during our marriage. And with each move, the number of book boxes grows. I collect cookbooks, he collects westerns, we collect anything and everything historical in nature from crafts to presidential history... to regional history.

However, during our last move, there was a box of cookbooks I couldn't part with. They were subsequently left in the storage unit. A year later when I had carved out a place for the remaining cookbooks, I discovered they had all become ruined with mold.

In my desire to save, I had lost. A hard lesson learned, but a productive one. The new rule is that titles only stay if there is room in our library or dedicated bookshelves.

Begin with asking some questions posed by HGTV... which will point you to a decision on whether it stays.

STEP 1: QUESTIONS

When was the last time I read this book?

Will I read it again?

If a reference book, is it current? If so, have I consulted it in the last year?

If it's a cookbook, do I use it? Hint: the presence of food stains indicates a keeper.

Is this a textbook from my old-school days?

Is the book a classic?

Does the book have intrinsic value — is it a signed copy, first or collectible edition?

Is the book out-of-print or hard to replace?

Is this a book I've borrowed and need to return?

STEP 2: SORT INTO COLLECTIONS

The books that will remain in your library need to be sorted by collection. As they are in a library.

Children's books belong on low shelves in the children's area or room

Reference books belong together (dictionaries, encyclopedia, and so on)

Separate novels and fiction works entirely. I like to categorize fiction by genre, keeping leather classics together and separating the rest. Locate in a library where it will be easy for you or a guest to find an interesting title on a rainy stay-at-home evening.

Non-fiction books need to be categorized by subject, as in a library. The goal is to find subject matters quickly, whether that be politics, travel, history, biography and so on.

STEP 3: CREATE STORAGE

Dedicate an area in your home to your main library. If you don't have built in shelves, create a library with freestanding bookshelves available at all home stores or online at Amazon.com and others.

CHECKLIST

Objective: to create a usable and organized home library that contains your resources.

☐ Begin with magazines and sort into piles — a keep, a donate, and a trash/recycle.

☐ Immediately eliminate those slated for recycling and box up the donations. Make a plan as to when you'll donate these items.

☐ Create storage for magazines you plan to keep and organize by collection, and then year, and finally by month. Place in designated area.

☐ Books. Gather books from around the house that aren't currently in a bookshelf or library. Bring them to the location where your central library will be or is located.

☐ Determine which books will be kept, and which will be donated.

☐ Organize remaining books by subject, as in a library.

☐ Clean and thoroughly dust shelves and books that will be re-organized back into the library.

☐ Organize books into newly cleaned shelves.

☐ Place children's books in the children's area, and set a couple of favorite books you plan to read on a nearby table. Plan a night in the near future to sit by a fire or drink a cup of tea and dive into your reading material and thoroughly enjoy your newly organized library.

TOMORROW

Medicine Cabinet

BOOKS AND MAGAZINE ORGANIZATION IDEAS

Vintage American Home, The New York Times, The Crowned Goat

DAY 27: MEDICINE CABINET

OBJECTIVE: MEDICINE CABINET

If you've ever rummaged through your medicine cabinet searching for headache relief and come up with only empty bottles and expired prescriptions, you know how important it is to keep your medicine cabinet organized.

It's been said that medicine cabinets are merely closets... in miniature.

And closet organizers have a simple rule they follow, each and every time.

We'll look at some helpful advice, apply the same organization techniques we've applied to every other area of our home, and look forward to a fresh, clean and organized medicine cabinet — where yes, everything will have a home.

HOW TO ORGANIZE MEDICINE CABINETS

So how do you find a place for everything and keep everything in its place in a medicine cabinet? Well, follow the same advice closet organizers have been selling for years: Get rid of anything you're not using. "Most of us are pack rats," says designer Lori Carroll of Lori Carroll and Associates in Tucson. "Go through the medicine cabinet every six months and throw out stuff you don't use. That means discarding tubes of used-up lipstick, rusty nail files and empty Band-Aid boxes."

1. PRIORITIZE

Medicine cabinets are only so big. It's important to keep only items in the medicine cabinet you use regularly. Keep occasional use items, like hydrogen peroxide or aloe in another location, drawer or under the sink.

2. DETERMINE TO STAY ORGANIZED

Resist the urge in stuff more little bottles into the medicine cabinet in a rush to clean up after a hectic morning. It will multiply faster than you can imagine.

3. PRESCRIPTIONS

Prescription drugs are not advised to keep in a medicine cabinet because humidity and heat can cause some to lose potency. Consider finding another location.

4. FIRST AID

In *"Reorganizing Your Medicine Cabinet,"* an online article from HGTV, they advise, "Keep your first aid supplies together so you can find them easily in case of an emergency. You might consider reserving one shelf for emergency supplies such as aspirin, first aid cream and gauze. Or buy a small emergency kit to keep on the medicine cabinet shelf and store the larger boxes of Band-Aids and tubes of antibiotic creams in the linen closet."

5. ORGANIZE

Organize items by use. Everyday items, including toothbrushes, should be at eye level. Infrequent use items should be organized on a higher shelf. Repackage bulky items into small containers (cotton balls, q-tips, etc.). Maximize space by using shelf risers and grouping like items together. Small tubes should be in small upright containers.

CHECKLIST

Objective: *to reclaim the medicine cabinet for healthcare and first aid items*

- ☐ Completely empty contents of the medicine cabinet.

- ☐ Wipe out the cabinet, clean and sanitize all surfaces.

- ☐ Sort through products and discard any expired, empty or unusable products.

- ☐ Create usable containers for items that will remain, eliminate bulky packaging on frequently used items so it fits in the cabinet — *see Inspirations below for ideas.*

- ☐ Determine if there is another location for prescription drugs.

- ☐ Inventory the cabinet and make a note of any items that will need to be replaced soon.

TOMORROW

Meal Planning

MEDICINE CABINET ORGANIZATION IDEAS

Container Store, Good Housekeeping

DAY 28: MEAL PLANNING

OBJECTIVE: MEAL PLANNING

That age-old question of "What's for dinner?" can be downright stressful at times. Especially on hectic nights when the household needs to be in 13 different places, at the same time. And everyone's hungry — at the same time.

Of course, I'm overstating. Usually it's not 13. But it feels like that sometimes.

The question itself doesn't cause stress. It only causes anxiety if you've nothing planned. Or at least a couple of options up your sleeve.

Which is exactly why I meal plan. I recently wrote an article on specifics of meal planning and what's worked for me. You can read that article online at www.31daily.com if you'd like.

http://www.31daily.com/simply-solving-the-whats-for-dinner-dilemma-a-meal-plan/

SIMPLE TIPS FOR MEAL PLANNING

1. KEEP IT SIMPLE

Especially if your new to meal planning, or even if you're a veteran, keeping the plan simple ensures the likelihood of following your plan.

2. PAIR DOWN THE INGREDIENTS

For busy nights, choose recipes that have few ingredients or are pantry staples.

3. THEME NIGHTS

Adopting theme nights your family likes is an easy way to remember and implement quick meals; Meatless Monday, Taco Tuesday, and so on.

4. CONSULT SOURCES

Several go-to websites have weekly meal plan ideas.

- **My Recipes Meal Planner:**
  http://www.myrecipes.com/menus/weeknight-meal-planners

- **Betty Crocker 30 Days of Dinner:**
  https://www.bettycrocker.com/register/30-days-of-dinner

- **Cooking Light Weeknight Meal Planner:**
  http://www.cookinglight.com/weeknight-meal-planner

- **Mayo Clinic Diet Meal Plan:**
  http://diet.mayoclinic.org/diet/mayo-clinic-diet-menu

- **Whole Foods Market Healthy Eating Meal Plans:** http://www.wholefoodsmarket.com/healthy-eating/meal-plans

- **All You Affordable Family Favorites:**
  http://www.allyou.com/food/celebrations/easy-delicious-meals

- **31 Daily Recipes:** http://www.31daily.com

5. DOUBLE-BATCH

Double-batch cook when possible. For instance, if you're serving lasagna one night, it's just as easy to make two. One for now, one for later. If you purchase a rotisserie chicken one night, buy 2, serve one for dinner, shred the second and freeze. Perfect for soups, enchiladas, salads and so much more.

6. ORGANIZE

Organize a space to meal plan. The Control Center is the perfect location for meal planning. Calendars and schedules are located there. Keep an indexed recipe card file for tried and true recipes your family loves, a binder for recipes you've printed from the internet and want to try — or recipes you're creating yourself. Stock at least 10 copies of a meal planning calendar and create a list of "family favorites," for quick reference.

Schedule a specific time and day to meal plan. The more you do it, the easier and quicker it will become.

CHECKLIST

Objective: *to create a meal planning center, stocked and ready for meal plans*

☐ Decide where you want to meal plan. Create a tab in your working files in the area and label it meal plans.

☐ Locate your recipe card file, a couple of cooking magazines you refer to often, and internet recipes you've printed and want to try.

☐ Print off at least 10 blank calendars or meal planning calendars. **Example at**: http://www.31daily.com/wp-content/uploads/2016/08/31Daily-Weekly-Dinner-Planner.pdf

☐ Create a "Family Favorite" list of meals. **Example at**: http://www.31daily.com/wp-content/uploads/2016/08/31Daily-Favorite-Meals-Printable.pdf

☐ Schedule a day and time that works best for you to meal plan. Sunday afternoons might work great.

☐ Plan a meal!

TOMORROW

Vehicles

DAY 29: VEHICLES

OBJECTIVE: VEHICLES

Vehicles are our home away from home, a traveling office whether you're a stay-at-home-mom, grandparent or student.

And just like an office, or our home, maybe even more so since it seems we are constantly in them, they must be organized and functional.

The best news is... the steps are easy.

EASY STEPS TO ORGANIZE YOUR VEHICLE

1. ELIMINATE

Take everything out of your car, toss garbage, empty bottles of Prell, yesterday's latte cup, empty wrappers and so on.

Pile everything into a box or bin that is presently in the vehicle and that you plan to keep.

2. CLEAN AND VACUUM

Thoroughly clean and vacuum every inch of the vehicle, including the trunk and between the seats. And while you're at it, anything that is removable, take out and clean like drink holders, etc. Clean the windows too.

3. ORGANIZE

Children:

For vehicles carrying precious cargo — children — place seat-organizers with their favorite car toys, books and travel games.

Glove Compartment/Console:

Store owner's manual, vehicle registration, auto club number, flash light, notepad and pen, tire gage, napkins, hand sanitizer, alcohol wipes, and other needed items.

Organizing expert Peter Walsh also recommends in "Tips for Organizing Your Messy Car":

Emergency Kit:

Purchase or make an emergency kit for your vehicle and store it in the trunk or the rear of the car. Include booster cables, a tire gauge, flares, reflective tape, a help sign, a screwdriver, pliers, a first aid kit, work gloves, a blanket, an old towel or rags, a jug of water and motor oil.

Survival Kit:

Put together a survival kit, especially if you live in a cold-weather climate. Include candles, waterproof matches, energy bars or candy bars, large plastic garbage bags and rubber bands. Keep larger items, such as cat litter (for slippery roads), a collapsible shovel, an extra blanket and heavy socks, hats and mittens (enough for several passengers), in a duffel bag or tub in the truth or rear of the car.

CHECKLIST

Objective: *to organize the vehicles and provide needed equipment while eliminating clutter.*

- ☐ Remove everything from the vehicle including the trunk, consoles and glove compartment. Discard trash and eliminate anything that isn't needed, or broken, or belongs somewhere else.

- ☐ Everything that will remain in the vehicle, put in a bin and set aside.

- ☐ Thoroughly clean and vacuum the vehicles – corners, trunk, under the seats – between the seats, the windows.

- ☐ Assemble car seat organizers for children, emergency kit and survival kit.

- ☐ Organize glove compartment and console.

- ☐ Take a pleasure ride!

TOMORROW

Calendar

DAY 30: CALENDAR

OBJECTIVE: CALENDAR

"He who every morning plans
the transactions of that day
and follows that plan
carries a thread that will guide him
through the labyrinth
of the most busy life."

— Victor Hugo

Time flies. We're all aware of that.

And if we're not careful, it gets away from us all too quickly. There is nothing worse than at the end of a tiring day to find you've accomplished nothing of what you'd planned or needed to do.

As we all know, some of those days are simply unavoidable. Life happens, after all. But when it becomes chronic, it's time to take a step back, look at not only our calendar, time management, but also our priorities. It's time for... a plan.

EASY STEPS TO ORGANIZE YOUR CALENDAR

1. TAKE A STEP BACK

Lou Gerstner, former CEO of IBM, once said: "Never let anyone own your schedule."

Take a moment and reflect on your week. Who or what was in control of your calendar last week? What activities required the largest chunks of time? Was it productive? Did it accomplish your goals?

Make a list of goals and commitments and determine which are the most important, including work, school, family, personal time, social time and any other commitments.

2. CREATE YOUR CALENDAR

Find a calendar system that works easily for you. If it isn't easy, it won't get done. Whether it's a paper calendar, a planner or a Cloud app on your phone — or even all 3.

3. PLAN YOUR WEEK

Routine:

"No matter what you are working on, create a routine. Block times for specific activities, and stick with the plan. Turn your calendar into a bunch of blocks, and put activities into those blocks. Whatever is not planned, you don't do. If you want free time, plan it," advises Alex Iskold of Entrepreneur Magazine.

Create Blocks of Time:

Begin by blocking out chunks of time for activities you do every day. Think about chunks of 15-30 minutes of back-to-back activities that you can pre-schedule. For example, block time for your priorities: exercise, study, personal development, email, family, etc. Be sure to include planning time; either daily or weekly whichever works for you.

Schedule Flex Time

As mentioned earlier, life happens. It doesn't always work the way we've scheduled it. To compensate, schedule flex time before and after events periodically throughout the day. By doing this, you can manage the unexpected and still accomplish your goals.

CHECKLIST

- ☐ Create a calendaring system that will work for you and will be easy to maintain.

- ☐ Plan a time when you can regularly update and manage your calendar.

- ☐ Input this week's schedule into calendar and if you have time, the month or beyond.

DAY 31: TAKE A WALK

Congratulations!

Today ends 31 days of reclaiming your home and your life, establishing order and eliminating clutter.

It was a worthwhile journey, a hopefully life-changing path that will produce a simpler, easier life. We've accomplished a lot together!

We will end our Easy Steps to an Organized Life the way we began – we will take a walk.

I encourage you to retrieve your notes from Day 1 and carry them with you as you once again tour your home and review your accomplishments. Remind yourself of what was, and appreciate what is… and even what could be.

You may want to take photos of the areas for which you are most proud, or where you made the biggest changes. Enjoy it! You've set a new course not only for yourself but for those you live with.

For the last 31 days, you decided to free your home from the unneeded stress of clutter and disorganization. It has been a journey that has put your eyes on every space in your house, from the entry way, to bedrooms, the kitchen, to closets, even the junk drawer. I hope the journey has been as meaningful to you as it has been to me!

WHAT YOU'VE ACCOMPLISHED

You have created a blueprint that will sustain what you've accomplished in the last 31 days. A blueprint that will carry you month in and month out as you manage home and simplify your life.

COMPLETING THE CYCLE

"It's exactly the same with the rest of your home. If you don't finish the task you commence, telling yourself, 'I'll get to that later,' then – in that moment – you've given into clutter. Finishing the cycle means completing anything that you start." – Peter Walsh

A FINAL THOUGHT

I have come, not willingly I might add, to the conclusion that we can reshuffle the chairs on the deck of the titanic any number of ways, but the ship is destined to sink unless we make changes in our life. Not a fan of the one-in, one-out theory of organization, as it seems arbitrary to me. There is, however, an underlying principle that remains. We can only reshuffle our "things" so many times before we realize that to stay truly organized and relieve our lives of stress, we must continue to eliminate.

Because truly, life is so much more than the sum of our possessions. Our "things" will never bring us the joy we desire. They are temporal at best. While they may bring joy for a moment, it won't last. As I mentioned in the beginning of this journey, "Things can be representative of moments in which we found joy, people who have brought joy, events that have brought joy. But the object itself does not bring joy."

While we have spent the last 31 days focused on eliminating and reorganizing, lasting joy is only found in the people we love, and the relationships we build.

Hopefully, what we've accomplished in the last 31 days will allow us to focus more fully on the people in our lives that matter most.

WELL DONE!

When we began this journey... our vision was to create a functioning plan, customized just for you. An adjustable plan that can be tweaked as life or addresses change. An organizational method you'll want to revisit time and again.

And your life?

Clear, purposeful... organized. We did it!

No plan is perfect, but we now have the basis to keep command of our "things" so our time can be spent enjoying the people and experiences that mean the most.

Here's to *keeping* an organized life – in 31 days or less!

CHECKLIST

Today I am including one last checklist to consider as a monthly blueprint. I use it as a daily reminder to spend a few moments areas of my home, put my eyes on the space and:

- ☐ Straighten as needed.

- ☐ Put away things that belong in other rooms.

☐ Eliminate as needed.

☐ Replenish as needed.

For Online Resources and to download printable checklists for "Easy Steps to an Organized Life in 31 Days," visit 31daily.com here:

http://www.31daily.com/easy-steps-organized-life-checklist-online-resources/

For informative daily articles – visit
www.31daily.com

We'd love to have you stop by!

NOTE FROM THE AUTHOR

 Thanks for reading, *"Easy Steps to an Organized Life in 31 Days"*! I'm Stephanie and I've been writing since I could hold a crayon between two fingers — left fingers that is.

I've been blessed with an amazing husband of more than 25 years and a now teenage son who keeps our life hopping! Oh — and he's super tall — and super sweet. But I'll stop at that. You know how moms love their kids.

A Northwest native by birth, I adore where we live, exploring the incredible natural beauty surrounding us. And while I love where I live, I also love to explore different regions of the world: the food, the culture, natural habitat – the history! Our family are lovers of history, which somehow threads through much of what I write. And I'm proud to say we've passed it down to the next generation through our son.

But most importantly, I love home. It's an adage, "Home is where the heart is," but it's incredibly true. Everything in my life centers around home. No matter the address, or how often it changes. It's a base, a welcome center, a safe place. I want it to serve as a peaceful haven, a respite from the crazy world in which we live.

When asked what I write about... I most often answer, "home." Whether that writing is fiction, genealogy, recipes, organization or family life. It's all about creating a beautiful space around us and nurturing those we get to claim as family and friends.

Thank you for being one!

Stephanie

ABOUT THE AUTHOR

Stephanie Wilson is a Northwest native. She has produced nationally syndicated television programs for CBS affiliates and has produced a television series which won a national Angel Award for excellence in the media. In addition, she has written news copy for a local CBS affiliate and directed marketing programs and special events for successful humanitarian organizations.

She earned two degrees from Seattle Pacific University in history and in communications.

Stephanie lives an active life in the Northwest and enjoys many hobbies during rare quiet moments, including; tennis, skiing, photography, gardening, knitting, spinning fibers, quilting, researching, genealogy, cooking, piano... and the list goes on. She also is actively involved in church, humanitarian organizations, community organizations, as well as other volunteer work.

Stephanie lives with her husband and son in a community near Seattle, Washington.

Visit Stephanie Wilson's website at
http://www.stephaniewilson.com

And read her daily articles at
http://www.31daily.com.

Made in the USA
Monee, IL
14 March 2023

29886627R00121